D1101194

THE WHICH? BOOK OF

Home Improvements

THE WHICH? BOOK OF

Home Improvements

MIKE LAWRENCE

WHICH?
BOOKS

CONSUMERS' ASSOCIATION

About the author

Mike Lawrence is a well-known writer in the field of do-it-yourself and home improvement. He has written several books for *Which?*, including *Which? Way to Fix It, The Which? Book of Wiring and Lighting, The Which? Book of Do-It-Yourself* and *The Which? Guide to Home Safety and Security.*

Which? Books are commissioned and researched by Consumers' Association and published by Which? Ltd, 2 Marylebone Road, London NW1 4DF

Distributed by The Penguin Group:
Penguin Books Ltd, 27 Wrights Lane, London W8 5TZ

First edition October 1996
Copyright © 1996 Which? Ltd

British Library Cataloguing in Publication Data
A catalogue record for this book is available from the British Library

ISBN 0 85202 611 0

Design by Sarah Watson
Cover design by Paul Saunders

Printed and bound in Great Britain by Scotprint Ltd, Musselburgh

All the photographs in this book have been reproduced by arrangement with **Houses & Interiors**, except those supplied by:

Steve Bielschowsky – pages 80, 96, 116, 122, 152
Gardening Which? magazine – pages 6 (bottom), 145
Sally and Richard Greenhill – pages 84, 85 (top), 86 (both)
The Robert Harding Picture Library
– cover photographs; main picture on the title page; pages 88, 90, 92
David Markson – pages 7, (top), 37, 79, 94, 104, 109, 154, 155 (bottom)
Marshall Cavendish Picture Library – pages 108, 146, 148 (both), 149 (all)
RICA – pages 63 (plugs), 65 (bath seat)
Which? magazine – pages 62, 63 (ironing board), 64, 65 (WC)

For a full list of Which? books, please write to Which? Books, Castlemead, Gascoyne Way, Hertford X, SG14 1LH.

Home Improvements

CONTENTS

* All organisations that appear in the book with an asterisk against their names appear in this address list

INTRODUCTION

*M*ost people spend their entire lives in other people's houses. A fortunate few have the opportunity to design and build their own dream homes, planning everything down to the last detail to suit their needs and lifestyles. Everyone else must live in a house that someone else built, altering and improving what they have acquired in order to call it, with justifiable pride, 'home'.

Improving the home is not a twentieth-century phenomenon. Every ancient archaeological site or old building reveals traces of its previous occupants' attempts to transform their surroundings for the better, and current home improvers are merely following in their footsteps by knocking rooms together, adding a conservatory, or putting in an extra bathroom. The end result may be a house that its original builder would barely recognise, but it will at least be what the new owner wants.

Apart from this desire to stamp their identities on the buildings they occupy, everyone is subject to external market forces. The recent slump in the housing market has made moving house extremely difficult for many people, so the only way of creating their ideal living conditions is to stay put and improve their existing home.

The Which? Book of Home Improvements helps you do precisely that: to make the best use of what you already have. It is not a do-it-yourself book as such, but covers everything you need to know about a range of home improvement projects, so that you get the end result you want, at a price you can afford, with or without professional assistance. ▶

Part 1 tells you how to assess your needs. To get your home to function in the way you want, you must begin by analysing how you use it at present, so that you can identify what works for you and what does not.

Part 2 is all about planning what to do once you have completed your initial assessment. It outlines what is involved in changing the way in which you use existing rooms, such as rearranging existing room layouts and access routes, 'borrowing' unused space within the house, adding new living accommodation, making better use of the site itself, and improving the service amenities, so making the house more energy-efficient and easier to maintain.

Part 3 looks at where to turn for professional help in realising your dreams of home improvement. It explains the services that architects, surveyors, consultants and specialist installers can offer, whether you want them to do just the design work, or to supervise the whole project.

Part 4 deals with getting official permission (if this is needed) for any improvements that you want to carry out. It explains the requirements of the Town and Country Planning Acts, the Building Regulations, and any other rules that may affect what you do and how you do it.

Part 5 will help you to decide who should do the work. It shows you how to break a project down into stages so that you can make sensible decisions about whether it is wholly a DIY job, one to leave to specialist contractors, or one that needs specialist input with only a modicum of DIY preparation or finishing.

Part 6 covers the whole question of cost. It explains how to work out a budget for a DIY project, and how to get estimates and detailed quotations from specialist contractors. It includes information on setting realistic timescales for the completion of projects, and gives advice on the logistics of buying materials and hiring tools and equipment. It also considers the best ways of raising the money for the project if its cost will exceed your resources.

Part 7 explains the importance of contracts, and warns about the hidden dangers contained in the small print of the standard terms and conditions that many contractors use. It also advises on how to avoid possible disputes, and how to deal with them if they do arise.

Part 8 completes the preliminaries, with advice on how to minimise disruption and maintain a semblance of ordinary life during DIY projects as well as those involving outside contractors.

The second half of the book describes and illustrates **30 popular home improvement projects**, ranging from converting basements to knocking down walls. Each project is self-contained, enabling you to see at a glance exactly what is involved, and which materials, tools, equipment and technical skills are required for carrying it out.

The book ends with a list of addresses of trade and contractors' associations which may be helpful, either during the planning stages of your project, or in the search for suitable specialist contractors. Any organisation flagged with an asterisk* in the text appears here too. Also included is a glossary of technical terms, just in case you need them.

Part I
ASSESSING YOUR NEEDS

*I*f you are going to improve your home, you have to start by working out what needs attention. This is often glaringly obvious: you have more children than bedrooms, or the existing kitchen facilities would disgrace a Dickensian workhouse. With problems like these, the solution is equally straightforward: you need an extension or a loft conversion on the one hand, or a new kitchen on the other.

Sometimes the problem is less easy to solve: a particular room layout never quite seems to work, or the bathroom is always cold and damp. Here it can be more difficult to find the right solution, since there may be several options.

To identify what improvements your home needs, it helps to analyse its shortcomings in functional terms. The following pages will help you to do this.

How adaptable is your home?

Every home has to perform in different ways at different times: from hour to hour, from day to day, and in the longer term. The demands made on it vary from household to household but, generally speaking, the more people there are in the home, the more adaptable it has to be. Here are some key questions to ask yourself.

♦ Are there queues for washing facilities in the morning or at bedtime?

♦ Is there a jam of people in the kitchen on weekday mornings?

♦ How flexible are mealtime arrangements? Could some meals be eaten in the kitchen and others in the dining-room?

♦ Can everyone gather together comfortably in the living-room? Can they all see the television from where they are sitting?

♦ Is there somewhere safe for children to play, especially if they are small?

♦ As the children get older, will it be possible for them to have separate bedrooms? This is essential, for brothers and sisters especially.

♦ Is there enough room to entertain friends or relations, especially if you would like to invite them to stay overnight occasionally?

♦ Is there room for family members to pursue hobbies or play indoor games?

Is there room for privacy?

Many family activities require peace, quiet and privacy. Adults need to be able to get away from children so that they can talk, read or listen to their choice of music. Children need somewhere quiet to do their homework, or to entertain their friends without evicting the grown-ups from the main living area.

Here are some more questions about how well your house measures up.

♦ Are children's bedrooms equipped for use as studies?

♦ Could the parents' bedroom be used as a retreat, with some comfortable seating, a television and hi-fi equipment?

♦ Could the dining-room be used as a second living-room, whether for work or entertaining?

♦ Is there another downstairs room that could do double duty as a children's playroom or an adults' sitting-room?

How well does the house's layout work?

You will get a good indication of whether your house is well designed, and whether you make good use of the space within it, by the amount of walking about you do each day. Ask yourself the following questions.

♦ Are any rooms accessible only via another room?

♦ Is the only WC upstairs? Is it located in the family bathroom?

♦ Is the kitchen planned to keep the work triangle – the route you have to take between the food storage and preparation area, the cooking area and the washing-up area – as small as possible?

♦ Is the dining area reasonably close to the kitchen?

♦ Are crockery, cutlery and glassware stored conveniently close to where they are needed on an everyday basis?

♦ Are bedrooms occupied by small children close to their parents' room?

How convenient is the access to the house?

Getting in and out of the house easily is just as important as getting around inside it. Your answers to the following questions will reveal how well your home performs in this respect.

♦ Is the approach to your front door easy to negotiate, especially if you are carrying shopping or luggage, or manoeuvring a baby buggy? Are there steps to negotiate? If so, are they shallow and wide, or steep and narrow?

♦ Is there shelter from the weather at the front door for you or any callers?

♦ Is there room in the hall for people to pass through easily? Can you shut the door if there are people in the hall?

♦ Is there room for hats and coats in the hall?

♦ Can you get to the back garden without passing through the living-room?

♦ Can you get to the back garden without passing through the house?

♦ Is there easy access from the house when you need to go to the washing line, the dustbin or the fuel store?

♦ Can rubbish be collected or fuel delivered when you are not at home?

♦ Is the car-parking space or garage conveniently close to the house?

How do individual areas perform?

Apart from the general questions listed above, you should also look at each room in turn and ask yourself how well it does its job.

♦ Does it have enough room to accommodate the necessary furniture and fittings in an arrangement that allows its occupant(s) to move about freely, open doors and windows, and otherwise use the room in an efficient manner?

♦ Is it well lit, heated, ventilated and, if necessary, soundproofed?

♦ Can you clean the windows easily?

♦ Could the room have any alternative uses – at weekends, for example, or as the family grows up?

♦ Are there any hidden dangers in the room, especially if it will be used by children, elderly or disabled people?

What about fixtures and fittings?

Improving the standard of the fixtures, fittings and services in your home could make a major contribution to enhancing your quality of life. This applies particularly to favourite home improvement areas such as the kitchen, the bathroom, the external doors and windows, and the heating system. You may want to replace fittings because they are damaged or unsafe, expensive to use or maintain, or simply because they look worn or outdated. Whatever the reason, it gives you an opportunity not just to replace like for like, but also to upgrade specification or performance.

Are there any special requirements?

If you have a disabled member of the family, or want to provide a home for an elderly relative, your house may need a variety of special provisions in order to cope with their requirements. These could include adapting access routes into and out of the house, fitting special equipment in the kitchen, bathroom and bedroom, or even installing a stairlift or through-floor lift. You will generally need professional help in planning such changes.

Do you work from home?

More and more people are choosing to work from home. If you are one of them, you will be faced with the problems of finding a workspace either within your home or in its environs. The size and type of space needed will obviously depend on the sort of work you do, but your primary aim must be to make a space that is clearly separate from the family parts of the home, so that you can work uninterruptedly and do not interfere with the family's domestic life any more than is strictly necessary.

SUMMARISING YOUR NEEDS

By now you will have a much clearer idea of what sort of improvements your home needs: more living space (or the better use of what you have), better access, better services and amenities, better energy efficiency, or even better use of the site as a whole. The next step is to put the required changes into some order of priority, and then to work out whether each improvement is possible. The following section of the book looks at the available options in greater detail.

Part 2
DECIDING
WHAT TO DO

*O*nce you have identified which areas of your home you want to change, the next
step is to work out the best way of making them better. The most common
home improvements can be divided into eight main types, and this chapter gives
a broad outline of what each involves, so that you can see whether it might be the solution
to your problems. Any of them could fit your requirements individually but you may need
to combine elements of several in order to get the end result you want.

CHANGING THE WAY YOU USE EXISTING ROOMS

Every room in your home currently has its own specific function. The house may have been built that way, or may have evolved its present layout as successive owners adapted it to suit their particular lifestyles. However, it need not stay as it is if it does not suit you. Here are some of the options you might like to consider.

♦ Turn the main living-room into a large kitchen-diner, leaving the existing dining-room and kitchen to act as separate living-rooms – one for home entertainment, perhaps, and one as a quiet room for reading or homework.

♦ Swap round the functions of the existing living- and dining-rooms, or swap ends if the activities of both occupy a large through-room.

♦ Strip out the built-in kitchen units that you do not need so that you can create space in the room for a dining area, thus freeing the existing dining-room to be used as an extra bedroom or living-room.

♦ Swap bedrooms to enable growing children to use a larger room for study and recreation; parents could just sleep in a smaller room.

♦ Turn a seldom-used spare bedroom into a children's playroom, a hobbies room or a home office.

♦ Fit out the boxroom as a second bathroom.

♦ Consider living upstairs and sleeping downstairs, especially if it gives you more sunlight and a better view.

For the most part, a room's change of use involves little more than rearranging the furniture; there is no structural work involved. If a kitchen or bathroom is being created or relocated, the job may involve rerouting services, but this need not create any insurmountable problems. You may need Building Regulations approval for the work, however, and you should also check whether planning permission is required if you intend to work from home. See Part 4 for more details.

REARRANGING EXISTING SPACE

Changing the layout of your house is rather more radical than simply changing the use to which you put individual rooms. It will not significantly increase the floor area, but may help you to make better use of the existing space. Again, there are several options you could consider.

♦ Create fewer and larger rooms by knocking down internal walls. Making a through-living-and-dining-room is one popular alteration, but you could just as well combine the hall and living-room (as long as you have a porch or lobby, so that the front door does not open directly into the converted room). The kitchen and dining-room could be turned into a large kitchen-diner. Upstairs, two adjacent bedrooms could be converted into a large master bedroom, with spacious dressing and sitting areas.

♦ Change the size of adjacent rooms by removing the existing partition wall and then re-erecting it to provide one larger and one smaller room. This could allow you to convert, for example, two existing bedrooms into one large bedroom with an en suite bathroom.

♦ Create more smaller rooms by installing new partitions within large existing rooms, or by removing one partition between two rooms and erecting new partitions to divide up the resulting floor space into three separate areas instead of two. This latter option can also, of course, be used to create an extra bedroom or a second bathroom.

♦ Changing the position of door openings in internal walls may help create more useful space by altering traffic routes through the house, and allowing a more

effective arrangement of the furniture against the walls. In through-rooms a second door could be blocked off. It may also be worth considering rehanging doors so that they open a different way, or using sliding doors instead of hinged ones in those situations in which the latter take up precious floor space.

♦ Changing the position of external doors may also be worth considering, especially those giving access to the side or rear of the house. An outside door in a kitchen may well provide a useful route to the garden, washing line or dustbin, but the traffic through the room seriously compromises the way in which the kitchen works. French or patio doors in a living- or dining-room will restrict the way in which the furniture can be arranged, whereas a window would give greater freedom.

♦ Moving the staircase may make better use of the space on the floor from which it rises, but this option may prove impossible in some house layouts. A spiral staircase may seem an obvious space-saver, but this rarely offers a significant gain in floor area, and can pose problems of safety and access for children, elderly people and furniture removers.

Rearranging existing space involves some structural work, especially if the walls you want to remove are load-bearing. You must always seek professional advice (see Part 3) if your plans affect a load-bearing wall. However, timber-framed partition walls can be removed and erected with relative ease.

Any structural work within the home will need Building Regulations approval, but you will not need planning permission except, perhaps, if you want to create facilities for working from home. See Part 4 for more details.

ADAPTING EXISTING UNUSED SPACE

Most houses have one major area of unused space within their existing outer shell: the loft. Others may have a basement or cellar, and some an integral or attached garage, which could all be converted into new living space without the need to build out the house itself.

Loft conversions

Converting the loft is one of the most popular large-scale home improvements, and, if it is well planned and executed, can be both a practical and an aesthetically pleasing addition to the house. Unfortunately, over the years, many houses and bungalows have been horribly disfigured by loft conversions that may well provide valuable extra living space on the inside but are eyesores when viewed from the outside.

The feasibility of a loft conversion depends on a number of factors. The first concerns the way in which the roof was constructed. If it was traditionally built with rafters, ridgepole, purlins and struts, the conversion will generally be fairly straightforward. However, professional advice is still always necessary to ensure that the roof structure will not be dangerously weakened by the conversion work. If the roof was built using prefabricated trussed rafters, conversion will be more difficult, but not impossible if steel joists are used to carry the floor load, and the existing rafters are strengthened.

The second factor concerns the potential room height. The Building Regulations no longer stipulate a minimum ceiling height for loft conversions (it used to be 2.3m – about 7ft 6in – over half the available floor area), but you are unlikely to get approval for a room height of less than 2m (about 6ft 6in). If your roof slope is particularly shallow, there may simply not be enough height in the existing roof space, and you would have to consider building above the roof ridge

– something many local planning committees are most unlikely to allow.

The third factor concerns providing access to the conversion from the floor below. It may be possible to fit a new staircase above the existing stairwell, but the design of the roof may mean that there is not enough headroom unless a dormer is built over the stairwell. Siting the new staircase anywhere other than above the existing stairwell will take up valuable floor space, which is something to take into account when measuring the gain in net space that the conversion will provide.

Converting a loft is a potentially complex job, which most people prefer to leave to an architect and builder, or to a specialist firm. However, there are considerable savings to be made by tackling some, or all, of the fitting-out work yourself, once the structural alterations have been professionally completed.

You will need Building Regulations approval for a loft conversion, but planning permission is not generally required unless you live in a listed building, or are in a conservation area or an area of outstanding national beauty. Full details are given in Part 4.

Basement conversions

Nowadays houses are seldom built with basements, but they are a common feature in those (especially urban ones) built before World War I. Some basements

were never intended to be more than small storage cellars, and were generally built beneath only part of the house. Others are more sizeable and can offer excellent potential for conversion.

As with loft conversions, three main factors will affect the feasibility of the conversion. The first is damp: however well the basement was built, it is below ground level and will therefore be at risk from water penetration from all sides, as well as from below, especially in areas where the water table has risen over the years. You may have to carry out extensive and potentially expensive damp-proofing treatment as the first stage of the conversion.

The second factor is that of ventilation, which must meet Building Regulations requirements if the basement is to be turned into habitable rooms: living-rooms, dining-rooms, bedrooms, and kitchens you can eat in. You may be able to overcome the problem of lack of ventilation by creating an open well outside the basement and installing windows that open into it, but if this is not possible mechanical ventilation will have to be installed.

The third factor is lack of natural light. You may be able to provide this by installing openable windows for ventilation (see above); otherwise, you will have to rely on artificial lighting. In this case, the uses to which you can put the basement rooms may be limited by the Building Regulations requirement for openable windows in habitable rooms.

Converting a basement may be relatively simple if the rooms are free from damp, but the job can be fairly complex and expensive if you intend to use them as habitable rooms.

Garage conversions

An integral or attached garage offers obvious potential for conversion into extra living space, especially if there is already an access door leading into it from the house. Popular uses for garage conversions include a playroom for children, and a home office. The amount of work involved in carrying out the conversion depends on the purpose to which you will put it.

If all you want is a workshop, a home for kitchen appliances such as the freezer, washing machine or tumble drier, or space to enable the children to play table tennis or set up a model racetrack, then a coat of paint on the walls and an extension of your wiring and plumbing systems is all you need.

If it is to be a truly habitable room, however, the work involved will be much more extensive. The garage floor may not include a damp-proof membrane, and may be at a lower level than the house floor; it will also need insulating to bring it up to Building Regulations standards. Unless the garage is wholly within the house, the external walls will be of single-thickness brickwork, so they will have to be both insulated and dry-lined. In an attached garage, you will also have to put in a ceiling with insulation above it; the ceiling of an integral garage should already be well insulated.

Most garage conversions turn the garage-door opening into a large front window. You may also want to add other windows to the side or back walls, especially if you intend to partition the space within the conversion. If there is no access door, you will have to create a new opening at a convenient point in the house wall, which may take up space within the house itself.

Finally, you will have to extend the house's wiring to provide better lighting and some power points, and will have to consider how to heat the new rooms. If plumbing facilities are required, you will have to extend supply pipes and make arrangements for getting rid of waste water.

Converting your garage offers valuable extra living space without the need for major structural alterations. However, if you are likely to move in the future, bear in mind the effect of the conversion on the saleability of the house; most house buyers prefer to have a garage for the car, not the family. The space can, of course, be converted back to garage use fairly easily, if this is required.

ADDING NEW LIVING SPACE

If you need more living space than is actually available within your home, and none of the previous options solves your problem, you have little choice but to build on. A full-blown extension of one or two storeys is the obvious choice, although adding a conservatory at the back or side of the house is also a popular way of gaining an additional living room or recreational area.

Home extensions

How you extend your home will depend on several factors. The most critical is the availability of space on the site for the projected extension, and it is generally obvious what the options are. The most likely is an extension at the back of the house, but it can be very difficult to make the new work look like part of the original building – the ideal of any home extension. If there is space at the side of the house, an extension here can be blended with the existing structure much more easily, especially if it is given a pitched, rather than a flat, roof. Front extensions are generally not allowed by the planning authorities, unless the house is set well back from the road or is behind the building line with which the fronts of the neighbouring properties are aligned.

Assuming that you have room on site to extend your home, you must next decide what sort of extra space you need, since this will dictate the type of extension that you build. A single-storey rear extension is ideal for extending a kitchen or living-room, but if you need more bedrooms or an extra bathroom, a two-storey extension is a must (unless, of course, you live in a bungalow). This will generally be a brand-new structure, also providing extra ground-floor living space or an integral garage, although in some cases you may be able to add a storey to an existing side garage or single-storey extension if the foundations and structure are strong enough. When planning a two-storey extension, you will have to pay particular attention to organising the access arrangements in order to minimise any undue loss of space in the existing house.

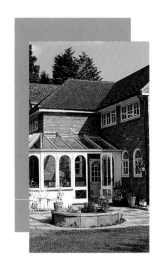

Once you have decided what to build and where to build it, you can start to plan the project in detail. The size of the job means that you will almost certainly need professional assistance from a designer, such as an architect, building surveyor or architectural consultant (see Part 3). Unless the work counts as permitted development, you will also need to apply for planning permission, and you will anyway need Building Regulations approval. See Part 4 for more details.

Conservatories

Conservatories have become one of the most popular types of major home improvements in recent years, reviving a construction that first attained fashionable status in Victorian times. In their current reincarnation they have evolved from the humble sunroom – essentially a lean-to greenhouse – into a variety of highly elaborate styles and shapes that are capable of blending in with any type of house design.

A conservatory is a specialised form of home extension, which you should consider if you want additional living space for general-purpose, everyday use, rather than extra bedrooms or a bigger kitchen. You are most likely to use one as an additional living- or dining-room, or as a separate playing space for children,

with the additional function of a garden room where you can grow indoor plants.

The modern conservatory is basically a modular building, consisting of a series of prefabricated glazed units which are assembled to form a perimeter wall that may be square, rectangular, or with angled corners in hexagonal or octagonal shapes. Full-length panels may have full- or half-height glazing; shorter panels are designed to sit on dwarf masonry walls, and may be chosen as an alternative to full-height panels, in order to make the conservatory look more like a part of the house than an addition. Double glazing is essential if you expect to be able to use the room all year round, as is good insulation in any solid-wall areas.

The roof is no longer the heavy structure of the traditional conservatories, with their panels of wired glass. Modern plastics technology has produced the perfect roofing material: a light, rigid sheet, with a box-section structure, which is available in twin- and triple-wall versions. The air trapped within the box sections acts as an excellent insulator, and the lightness of the material, coupled with its strength, means that the roof structure can also be comparatively light in weight and unobtrusive in appearance.

A conservatory is usually sited at the back of the house, for obvious reasons: it will act as an extension to the main living areas, and the back is where space is most likely to be available. However, if there is room, it could also be sited at the side of the house, and such a position will maximise the effects of the available sunlight. A front-sited conservatory is less likely to receive planning consent unless your house is set well back from the road, but this need not rule it out entirely. You could even consider building your conservatory as a detached structure linked to the house by a covered walkway, if this solution suits the site and its aspect: for example, if the back of the house faces north and gets virtually no sun.

Adding a conservatory is generally one of the least disruptive types of home improvement to carry out, since all the construction work takes place outside the house. Most conservatories are built against walls which already have either an existing door opening, or a window that can be easily enlarged to form one. Once the base for the structure is in place, the building can be erected and weatherproofed in a day or so, and is then ready for immediate use.

Most people buy a conservatory from a specialist supplier who also carries out all the installation work, but an alternative is to order the components and assemble the building yourself.

Conservatories count as home extensions for planning purposes, so whether you need to apply for planning permission or not will depend on whether you have already used your permitted development allowance (see page 30). In England, Wales and Northern Ireland conservatories are exempt from Building Regulations control as long as they do not exceed 30sq m (about 325sq ft) in area; in Scotland there is no automatic exemption, so check before you build. See Part 4 for more details.

Porches

Adding a porch will not of itself provide any additional living space, but having one may allow you to reorganise the entrance hall and perhaps make more use of it as a room once its door no longer opens to the outside air. A porch will certainly improve your quality of life by cutting down draughts and improving your home's security, as well as its thermal and sound insulation. It will also act as a handy buffer zone between the house and the great outdoors, providing somewhere to leave muddy boots and wet coats, and affording shelter to callers and a secure area for doorstep deliveries.

For most types of house, an add-on porch will be the obvious solution. It can be a tailor-made mini-extension or a prefabricated structure. The latter is created by assembling off-the-peg window and door panels (similar to those of a conservatory), and then adding a flat or pitched roof. If your front door is recessed – a popular design feature of many 1930s semis – you can create an enclosed porch simply by installing a second door and frame standing flush with the house's wall.

Whichever option is chosen, the key to success lies in making the porch match the look of the existing house. This means using windows and doors of similar style, matching existing brickwork or rendering, and, if possible, shaping the roof to echo the style and covering of the house roof. A typical kit porch with a flat roof will always tend to look like an afterthought.

Small porches do not need planning permission. They are exempt from Building Regulations control in England, Wales and Northern Ireland, but need approval in Scotland. See Part 4 for more details.

MAKING BETTER USE OF THE SITE

The home improvements outlined so far have concentrated on the house itself, but there are several improvements you can make to the site itself, and to the way in which you use it. These include building a garage or carport, providing additional car-parking space, creating a new or better access route from the road, and putting up other outbuildings such as workshops, saunas, aviaries and swimming-pool enclosures.

Garages and carports

If you do not have a garage, or you have already turned an integral or attached garage into extra living space, then building a new one will both enhance the value of your property and provide cover and security for your car. You must have space on-site for it, of course, and you may also need to consider such aspects as altering the access route to the new garage from the road, or else extending an existing drive to reach it.

You can either build a garage from scratch, or buy and erect a modular, kit garage. The former will be more expensive, but does give you the opportunity both to match the building's appearance closely to that of the house, and also to accommodate any special requirements of your own.

Kit garages have the advantage of being very quick to erect, since once the base is in place you simply bolt the wall panels together, add the roof trusses, fix on the roof covering, and install the main door, along with any other doors and windows. They are available in single, double and twin versions, and their modular design means that you can easily extend the basic building, if you wish, to incorporate a workshop or storage area.

A garage built within 5m (16ft) of the house is classified as a home extension for planning purposes, so permission may be needed if your permitted development allowance has already been used for previous extension work. If it is further away from the house, it is classed as an outbuilding (see below), and you may not need planning permission. As far as Building Regulations control is concerned, garages are generally exempt. See Part 4 for more details.

Carports are a low-cost alternative to a garage, and are worth considering if space is not available for a full-sized garage. They can also provide shelter for a second car or caravan, either beside the house or garage, or between the two. You can easily build one yourself, erecting the masonry, steel or timber supports, and then adding a simple flat roof. Alternatively, you can buy prefabricated kits for do-it-yourself installation. A carport is treated as an outbuilding for planning purposes (see below), and is generally exempt from Building Regulations control.

Car-parking areas

Whether you have a garage or not, being able to park your car off the street is a benefit on grounds of both convenience and security. You can put down concrete or tarmac, lay paving slabs or interlocking-block paving stones, or just order a lorry-load of gravel if the site is flat. As long as any vehicle parked on the site is used primarily as a private car (not as a trade or hire vehicle), no official permission or approval is needed.

However, you will generally need planning permission if you want to create a new route for vehicles to your property from the road. If the new access route crosses a public footpath or verge, you will also need the consent of the local authority highway department.

Outbuildings

There is a wide range of outbuildings that you can erect in your garden for leisure purposes. These include garden sheds, greenhouses, sauna cabins, swimming-pool enclosures, children's playhouses and homes for birds and animals, such as aviaries, horseboxes and poultry houses. You can either build these structures yourself, using the appropriate materials, or else buy them in prefabricated form ready for erection on site; all need proper bases.

You can generally erect whatever you like by way of outbuildings on your property, although there are planning restrictions governing their size and location. It pays to consult your neighbours first if the buildings will be against their boundaries. You should also check to see whether any restrictive covenants are in existence on your property: for example, concerning keeping animals as livestock as opposed to family pets.

IMPROVING SERVICE AMENITIES

Unless your house is relatively new, it is highly likely that it would benefit from some improvements to its services: the plumbing, wiring and the heating system. Modern lifestyles make increasing demands on all three, and your existing services may be buckling under the strain.

The plumbing

Compared with the standard provisions of only a generation ago, modern households require more than just water in the bathroom and at the kitchen sink. You may want to install additional washbasins and shower cubicles at locations in the house other than the bathroom, fit a second WC, create a utility room with another sink, plumb in washing machines and dishwashers, fit a water softener, or add an outside tap. Even if you do not plan to do anything so extensive, you may still want to reorganise the existing plumbing arrangements as part of a kitchen or bathroom refit. The work may need Building Regulations approval as far as relocating waste water disposal is concerned, and must comply with the requirements of the water bye-laws affecting water supply. See Part 4 for more details.

The wiring

Our ever-increasing use of electricity is another potential area for improvement. Homes nowadays contain electrical equipment undreamt of a mere generation ago, all needing somewhere to be plugged in. Increasing numbers of home-owners are also discovering that there is more to lighting the home than having just a central pendant light in every room. Satisfying this demand may involve the extension of existing circuits, the provision of new ones, and even complete rewiring if the system is old and cannot stand the extra load. The work needs no official permission (except in Scotland), but should be carried out to Wiring Regulations standards – see Part 4.

The heating

Home heating is another area in which you may decide that you can make some worthwhile improvements. Modern boilers provide hot water and space heating far more efficiently than their predecessors, and their small size and versatility over where they can be sited means that they need no longer dominate the room in which they are fitted. Fully pumped systems offer faster response times than their gravity-driven forebears, and modern radiators are more efficient than ever. Bear in mind that the installation of new heating appliances needs Building Regulations approval, however.

IMPROVING ENERGY EFFICIENCY

Upgrading the heating system is one obvious step towards improving the energy efficiency of your home and cutting your heating bills. Others, such as incorporating improved thermal insulation, improving draught-proofing and providing controlled ventilation, are less obvious as visible home improvements. However, they should be part and parcel of many of your projects, whether you are converting the loft, fitting double glazing or replacing doors and windows, and they will all have long-term, cost-saving or comfort-improving benefits. Note that new building work will have to meet the thermal insulation requirements of the Building Regulations.

REDUCING FUTURE MAINTENANCE NEEDS

Every home-owner's dream is to live in a maintenance-free home. Many of the home improvements featured in this book give you the opportunity to plan for a future free from unnecessary maintenance and repairs by selecting materials and equipment that offer enhanced performance, longer life and, if they need maintenance at all, less hard work in keeping them in good order. So if your do-it-yourself schedules are dominated by painting the timber cladding every year, or regularly overhauling the bathroom taps, keep this point in mind when weighing up the options available to you.

THINKING OF MOVING?

Once upon a time, moving house was easy. You moved house if your job location changed; you moved to a bigger house if you needed more living space; you moved to a more expensive house as your earnings increased, in the sure knowledge that you would make a profit on your investment as house prices continued their inexorable rise. Not any more.

With a sluggish housing market, and low house-price inflation, deciding to stay where you are has become the logical choice for many people, and improving what you have the sensible alternative. For most people, moving to another house is very much the last resort, when all the possible home improvement opportunities have been exhausted.

Part 3

PROFESSIONAL HELP

*I*f you are an experienced do-it-yourselfer, you may feel able to plan and execute many improvement projects without the need for professional help. For all but the simplest jobs, however, many people will appreciate the inside knowledge that experts can bring to the project, especially when it comes to solving design problems, making the best use of existing space, and planning the best way of creating more of it. You will also need professional help for projects that involve structural alterations to the house, to ensure that new foundations, walls, load-bearing lintels and the like are strong enough to do their job. On a major project, unless you have extensive experience of building work, you may want to hand over the entire management of the job to the professionals, letting them deal with everything from the early design stages to getting official permission, awarding contracts and supervising the work.

ARCHITECTS

An architect can style himself or herself as such only if he or she is registered with the Architects' Registration Council*. Many architects are members of the Royal Institute of British Architects (RIBA)*, or of the parallel bodies in Scotland and Wales. You will find local architects listed in your *Yellow Pages* phone directory, and you can get the details of registered architects practising in your area from their professional bodies.

Just because someone is a registered architect does not mean that he or she will be the ideal person to deal with your home improvement project, however. Some architects specialise in new building work or the commercial sector only, and it is important to establish early on whether the person you have approached is both experienced in relatively small-scale domestic work, and is genuinely interested in taking on the project. Personal recommendation is one of the best ways of finding someone suitable.

Once you have found someone, it is important from the outset to have a clear idea of what you expect your architect to do for you. One of the main reasons why many architects do not like working for private individuals is that they are forever changing their minds, and do not expect to pay for the extra time spent coping with the constant changes.

What your architect will do for you

The first step will be to hold a brief preliminary meeting, often free, at which you can outline what your project involves. Depending on the type of project, it can help to take along photographs of the house and any sketches and plans that you have drawn. It is also important to discuss at this stage what level of involvement in the project you expect the architect to provide. The various stages involved in a typical home improvement project include:

♦ preliminary project-planning advice
♦ preparing drawings to your specifications
♦ submitting plans for local authority approval
♦ obtaining tenders for the work from contractors
♦ preparing contracts
♦ preparing work schedules
♦ supervising site work
♦ issuing certificates for payment.

The more of these services you use, the higher the final bill. Depending on the extent of supervision required, the architect's fee may be charged as a percentage of the total cost of the job or, if little involvement beyond the planning stage is required, as a flat fee based on the amount of time spent on the work.

Once you have agreed what you want done, how much involvement you expect, and what the fee will be, you should receive written confirmation of the relevant terms. If you do not, you should draw up a letter of appointment yourself, outlining exactly which duties you want performed.

SURVEYORS

Unlike architects, anyone can adopt the title of surveyor, and there are also several kinds of surveyor around, not all of whom are qualified in design and building work. You will need a building surveyor, and, as with architects, you can find one by contacting the relevant professional bodies, such as the Royal Institution of Chartered Surveyors (RICS)*, for lists of their members in your area. Alternatively, look in the *Yellow Pages* under 'Surveyors – building', or rely on personal recommendation.

A building surveyor will carry out roughly the same range of duties as an architect, and a RICS member or similarly qualified surveyor will make charges very similar to those of a registered architect.

CONSULTANTS

Apart from architects and qualified building surveyors, there are also many firms and individuals offering to do similar work, but lacking any official registration. They may call themselves architectural consultants, architectural surveyors or architectural technicians – in fact, anything but architects. They do not have to adhere to any professionally monitored codes of conduct, and may not have professional indemnity insurance to protect you against losses resulting from negligent design or survey work. However, the work they do may well be of a first-class standard (or not), and they will certainly charge less than an architect or qualified building surveyor. If one is recommended to you, and has the references to back up the recommendation, by all means consider using them.

LOCAL BUILDING CONTROL OFFICERS

Many smaller-scale home improvement projects do not warrant the employment of an architect, surveyor or other professional adviser, but may need to meet the requirements of the Building Regulations in one way or another. The individual

project checklists later in the book indicate when Building Regulations approval may be needed, but they cannot cover every eventuality, and the layman cannot be expected to know the detailed Regulations requirements. This is where local authority building control officers (BCOs) have a vital role to play.

BCOs are generally happy to give advice on what the Regulations require (as long as you do not overdo the questioning), and are aware that some helpful advice given while a do-it-yourself project is being planned can save both employer and contractor time and money later on if unacceptable plans or workmanship have to be rejected. They will also carry out site inspections, if appropriate, during the progress of projects not under the supervision of a qualified inspector such as an architect or building surveyor.

SPECIALIST COMPANIES

There are several types of home improvement projects that lend themselves to the approach of the package dealer, including loft conversions, conservatories, and bathroom and kitchen refits. Such companies offer to manage every step of the project, from initial design (nowadays often computer-aided) through to final completion, and this way of operating can seem very appealing if the alternative is to employ a range of professional advisers and separate contractors.

However, unless you take care to invite plans and costings from several such firms, and take the time to read the contract forms closely before you sign, you can find yourself at the mercy of the firm you have selected, without the back-up of any independent professional advice. As with any home improvement project, it is best to stick to those contractors that have been personally recommended to you, and who have satisfied local customers to testify for them.

HELPING YOURSELF

If you are planning, managing and running your own home improvement project, you can keep things going smoothly by paying the same attention to detail as a professional throughout the job.

Start by doing your homework thoroughly, researching the products and materials you intend to use, and the scope of the work involved.

Contact the technical services department of firms making the products that you are interested in using, and ask for their literature and advice, plus the details of local stockists.

Visit your local library, where you should find numerous specialist technical books on all aspects of building, woodworking, decorating, plumbing and electrical practices to help your home improvements project.

Contact product and trade organisations relevant to the project you have in mind. Many publish a range of helpful (and often free) literature, and will put you in touch with member firms who can provide further assistance if necessary.

Visit local trade merchant outlets, where you will be welcomed much more warmly than you might have been in the past. This will enable you to find out about trade products not available in the do-it-yourself sector, and to pick the brains of staff, who often have considerable expert knowledge which they are only too happy to share with a potential customer.

Part 4

GETTING PERMISSION

*A*s you will already have discovered, many home improvement projects require official permission or approval of one sort or another. Before you start work, it is your duty first to find out which rules and regulations are relevant to the job, and then to ensure that you either seek prior permission if this is required, or that the work you do complies with the rules once completed. This section looks at the requirements for certain individual projects in more detail.

Failure to comply with regulatory requirements can be expensive and there is little to gain in the long run by not doing so, especially where safety is a factor. You might save a little time and a bit of money now, but if your unsatisfactory work kills someone in the future, you might not feel quite so clever.

BUILDING AND PLANNING CONTROL

The two most important sets of rules affecting the way in which you carry out your home improvement projects are the Town and Country Planning Acts, and the Building Regulations. In brief, the former govern what your house looks like from the outside, what impact it makes on the street scene and the neighbourhood, and the uses to which it and the land on which it stands are put. The latter ensure that the building is structurally sound, and is safe and healthy to live in. Both have the force of law behind them, so ignore them at your peril.

Some home improvements require planning permission only; others need Building Regulations approval alone; some require both.

Ensuring that a project complies with Building Regulations requirements is relatively straightforward, since they are applied uniformly throughout England and Wales (Scotland and Northern Ireland have their own separate, but broadly similar, Regulations). All references given in this book refer to the Building Regulations in force in England and Wales at the time of publication. However, planning rules vary in interpretation, if not in principle, from one local authority to another, so the information given in this section should be interpreted in general terms only. Most local authorities publish guidelines for home-owners wishing to alter or extend their properties, and it is worth obtaining a copy of these if you are planning work of this sort.

What you will (or will not) be allowed to carry out to your property in planning terms is further complicated by the existence of what is termed 'permitted development'. This is intended to prevent local authority planning departments from being flooded by trivial planning applications, and allows certain types of extension and alteration work to domestic properties to go ahead, irrespective of the local authority's wishes.

Perhaps the best way of illustrating how planning rules and building controls affect what you can do is to consider them in the context of the projects described later in the book. What is involved in applying to your local authority for planning permission and Building Regulations approval if you need it is then dealt with in the subsequent section.

Building a home extension

First, the simple part: any home extension must comply with all the relevant sections of the Building Regulations, so you will have to apply for approval from your local authority (see **Applying for permission** – see page 34 – for full details of exactly what is involved).

Now for the complex part: permitted development allows home extensions to be built without the need to apply for planning permission, subject to certain restrictions, as follows:

♦ the extension must not increase the volume of the original house by more than the permitted volume allowance (see the box). The term 'original house' means the house as it was when it was first built, or as it stood on 1 July 1948 if it was built before then.

As long as it meets the permitted volume allowances outlined in the box, the extension will not need planning permission if it complies with the following additional conditions:

♦ it must not project above the original roof line of the house, nor in front of any house wall facing a highway
♦ it must not exceed 4m (13ft) in overall height if it will be built within 2m (6ft 6in) of a boundary
♦ it must not result in more than half the site being built on.

PERMITTED VOLUME ALLOWANCES

In a terraced house (or in any house in a national park, a conservation area, or an area of outstanding national beauty), the maximum volume of a permitted extension is either:

♦ 50cu m (1,765cu ft), or 10 per cent of the volume of the original house, whichever is the greater, up to a maximum of 115cu m (4,060cu ft).

For any other house, the maximum volume is:

♦ 70cu m (2,470cu ft), or 15 per cent of the volume of the original house, whichever is the greater, up to the same maximum of 115cu m (4,060cu ft).

In Scotland the permitted volume is 50 cu m, or 20 per cent of the volume, up to the same maximum allowance.

These are once-and-for-all allowances. Previous extension work to the property may have used up part, or all, of the permitted allowance, and, if this is the case, planning permission must be sought for the new work. The volume figures quoted include the volume contained beneath a pitched roof.

Note that if the extension is built to provide facilities such as a self-contained granny flat or a home office, planning permission may be needed to cover the change of use, even if the extension itself comes within the permitted development rules. Check this out at an early stage.

Remember, too, that there may be circumstances in which your permitted development rights have been removed: for example, as a condition of a previous planning consent, such as that granted when the house was first built.

Adding a conservatory

A conservatory is defined as having a transparent or translucent roof, and the structure itself is exempt from Building Regulations control as long as its floor area does not exceed 30sq m (325sq ft). However, certain sections of the Regulations still apply to its installation, as follows:

♦ safety glass must be used in doors and low-level glazing in the conservatory to comply with Part N of the Regulations

♦ structural alterations creating new access routes into the conservatory from the house must comply with parts A and L

♦ there must be ventilation openings (such as patio doors or french windows) in the conservatory, and in any habitable room that will be ventilated through it, to comply with Part F of the Regulations. The doors must have an opening area equal to 5 per cent of the combined floor area of the two rooms. In addition, each room must have background ventilation, with a minimum open area of 8,000sq mm (12sq in).

A conservatory is classed as a home extension as far as planning permission purposes are concerned, and the same criteria as contained in the permitted development rules apply. If it is a detached building more than 5m (16ft) from the house, it is classified as an outbuilding (see below).

Adding a porch

Permitted development rights, if not suspended, allow a porch to be built without the need for planning permission as long as:

♦ it has a floor area of 3sq m (32sq ft) or less

♦ it is no more than 3m (10ft) high

♦ it is situated at least 2m (6ft 6in) from any boundary between your property and a road or public footpath.

However, check with your local authority before building a porch if you live in a national park, a conservation area, or an area of outstanding national beauty, or if the house is a listed building.

Porches built under permitted development rights are exempt from Building Regulations control, except in the unlikely event that they exceed 30sq m (325sq ft) in floor area.

Converting a loft

Loft conversions always need Building Regulations approval in order to make sure that the alterations satisfy the requirements concerning structural stability, safe access, thermal insulation, ventilation, fireproofing, waste disposal (if the conversion will contain sanitary facilities), and, above all, means of escape in the event of fire. You must deposit full plans, not just a building notice, if you are converting a two-storey building.

Planning permission to create dormer windows on roof slopes above new loft rooms is not needed in England and Wales as long as the window does not face a road or project above the roof line. The installation of dormer windows always needs planning permission in Scotland.

Adding a garage or carport

If you build a new garage next to your house, or within 5m (16ft) of it, it is classed as a home extension for planning purposes, and permission will be needed unless the building falls within the relevant permitted development rules. Since most garages are relatively small in terms of volume, your project will most probably meet these criteria unless the house has already been extended in some way, and has thus used some, or all, of the permitted volume allowance.

If the garage is more than 5m from the house, it is classed as an outbuilding (see the section below), and the planning restrictions are far less onerous for this category (but note that in conservation areas and areas of outstanding national beauty, garages are always classed as extensions). Conversely, carports are treated as outbuildings, wherever they are sited.

Garages are exempt from Building Regulations control, provided that their floor area does not exceed 30sq m (325sq ft), and that they are either built entirely of non-combustible materials, or are sited at least 1m (3ft 3in) away from the property's boundary. Carports are also exempt, subject to the same floor area restrictions. They must also be open on at least two sides – otherwise they are classed as a doorless garage.

Providing off-road parking

Neither planning permission nor Building Regulations approval is needed to create a parking area for your car, as long as it is situated wholly within your garden, and your car is used primarily as a private vehicle (not as a trade or hire vehicle). You may need planning permission, however, if you need to create a new access route to the parking area from the road, and you will also need the consent of the local authority's highways department if the access route will cross a public footpath or verge (unless the road is unclassified).

Putting up outbuildings

You can erect a wide range of small outbuildings in your garden, such as sheds, greenhouses, and even swimming-pool enclosures, without the need to apply for planning permission, provided that:
♦ they are not for residential use
♦ they are not situated in front of the building line (the wall of the house facing the highway)
♦ they do not exceed 4m (13ft) in height if they have a pitched roof, or 3m (10ft) if they have a flat one
♦ building them will not result in more than half the garden being built on.

Building Regulations approval is not needed either, as long as the building has a floor area of 30sq m (325sq ft) or less, and is either built of non-combustible material, or is at least 1m (3ft 3in) from the property's boundary.

If you are planning to install a swimming-pool, you will need approval from your local water supply company; you can also expect a substantial increase in your water rates once it has been built.

Creating a through-room

Internal alterations such as creating a through-room do not need planning permission unless a change of use is being contemplated: to turn one or more rooms into a self-contained flat or a home office, for example.

However, you will need Building Regulations approval if the dividing wall that you are removing is load-bearing, to ensure that the alterations will be structurally sound. In particular, the lintel that will carry the superimposed load must be of the right type and size, must be installed correctly, and must be adequately fire-

proofed. You will need the advice of an architect, surveyor, qualified builder or building control officer on this point.

The Regulations also require the new room to be adequately ventilated, via windows with an openable area equal to at least 5 per cent of the floor area of the combined rooms. Part of the openable window must be at least 1.75m (5ft 9in) above floor level.

Partitioning a room

Again, planning permission is not needed for a project such as partitioning a room, although some requirements of the Building Regulations will have to be met, especially those concerning sound transmission between the two rooms and their ventilation requirements. As with through-rooms, each new room must have openable windows equal in area to 5 per cent of the room's floor area, and the rooms may not share an existing window opening. If the partitioning creates a room in which a window is not essential (a bathroom, for example), then you will have to provide mechanical ventilation by means of an extractor fan.

Converting an integral or attached garage

If your house has an integral or attached garage, you may want to turn it into additional living space, especially if you have enough room on site to build a new garage. The job may need Building Regulations approval, especially with regard to improving the thermal insulation of an attached garage, which will not have cavity walls or any roof insulation. It may also need planning permission if it is undergoing a change of use. Always check with your local authority before proceeding with the conversion, since some of them regard existing integral garages as being exempt from Building Regulations control.

Creating new door or window openings

If you are creating new door or window openings in external or internal load-bearing walls where none previously existed (as opposed to replacing existing doors and windows), you will need Building Regulations approval to ensure that the lintel used to span the new opening is of the correct type and size for the job, and that openings in external walls are correctly damp-proofed. You do not need approval to create openings in internal, timber-framed walls.

Altering your kitchen or bathroom

Building Regulations approval is not needed when altering a kitchen or bathroom if all you are doing is replacing the old equipment and fittings with new ones. If you are making any alterations to the existing waste-water disposal arrangements, however, or are fitting a heating appliance where none existed before, you will need approval for the new work.

You will also need approval if you are partitioning a WC from an existing bathroom, installing a second WC, or fitting washbasins or shower cubicles into bedrooms, because new waste pipes will have to be installed. In the case of new WC cubicles, the Regulations ventilation requirements must also be met. Remember that the Regulations now allow the use of a pumped macerator unit and small-bore pipework if the siting of the new appliances makes running conventional soil and waste pipes difficult.

Installing new heating appliances

You need Building Regulations approval if you plan to install any new fuel-burning appliance, or to construct a new flue, and also if you want to install certain

types of unvented heating systems in place of an existing vented system. These unvented systems are not suitable for do-it-yourself installation; they must be fitted only by approved installers. You may need planning permission to construct a new external chimney or flue, or to install a gas- or oil-storage tank on your property.

APPLYING FOR PERMISSION

If your proposed home improvement project clearly needs planning permission, Building Regulations approval, or both, contact your local authority planning and building control departments and ask them to send you the relevant forms, as well as any guidance notes they may publish to help you with your application. You will usually find the two departments bracketed together in the phone book, under the heading 'Technical services'.

If you are unsure whether you need official approval for your plans, make an appointment with the relevant department to discuss your proposals. The golden rule is: if in doubt, ask.

Planning permission

If you need to apply for planning permission, you usually have to fill in four copies of the application forms (or, if your time is too short to do everything in quadruplicate, one copy and three photocopies) and then send them to the planning department, accompanied by four copies of all the relevant drawings (including a site plan) and the appropriate application fee.

The local authority will consider your application, and will usually send you a decision notice within two months of the date of your application. Do not start work until you receive this. If permission is granted, it is valid for five years. If it is refused, and you consider that the refusal is unreasonable, you can appeal to the Department of the Environment (or the Welsh Office if you live in Wales) within six months of receiving the notice. You can also appeal in this way if you do not receive a decision at all within the two-month time limit.

Building Regulations approval

If you need to apply for Building Regulations approval, you have two possible courses of action. The first is to deposit a full set of all the relevant plans with your local building control office; the second is to give them what is known as a 'building notice', which has to be accompanied by (rather less) detailed information about the proposed work. Both methods of application must be accompanied by the relevant fee. Whichever course you take, you can begin work 48 hours after depositing the documents, but if you do this, you must be sure that your project will fully comply with the Regulations.

If you deposit full plans, you can wait for them to be accepted in writing if you prefer; the authority must give you a decision within five weeks, unless you agree to an extension of two months. This route at least gives you the written evidence that the work fully complies with the Regulations; with the building notice scheme you will receive only oral confirmation of compliance during the periodic inspections of the work that the building control officer will make.

OTHER CONTROLS ON DEVELOPMENT

Apart from the planning and building controls outlined above, your proposals may also have to comply with other legal requirements, such as local authority bye-laws (which may be in addition to, or at variance with, national rules), restrictive covenants on your property, and the rules for listed buildings or those in conservation areas or areas of outstanding national beauty. As with the planning and building rules, it is your responsibility to ensure that you are aware of these requirements before you start work, either by consulting your local authority or, in the case of restrictive covenants, with the help of a solicitor.

BREAKING THE RULES

If your local authority becomes aware that you have carried out work on your home without the prior necessary permission or approval, it is likely to take action against you. As far as a breach of planning requirements is concerned, you may be able to make a retrospective application for permission. You are more likely to receive an enforcement notice, however, requiring you to restore the property to its former condition or use, and you may also be prosecuted. Such notices must be issued within four years of the unauthorised development taking place; if they are not, no further official action can be taken against you.

If you carry out work that does not comply with the requirements of the Building Regulations, and this is discovered, you will initially receive an enforcement order giving you 28 days in which to correct the work in compliance with the Regulations. If you do not comply, the local authority may then undertake the necessary work itself, and then send you the bill. Alternatively, you may be fined a lump sum, plus an additional fine for every day during which you remain in default. However, the enforcement notices cannot be served more than 12 months after the work was originally completed.

If you carry out work that is in breach of a restrictive covenant on your property, your situation is much less clear-cut. Many properties accumulate a series of restrictive covenants under successive owners, and their requirements can last indefinitely. Some restrictive covenants are old, completely irrelevant to modern life, and are likely to be unenforceable; your solicitor will advise you on how to go about having them legally set aside. Others, often imposed on modern estates by

their developers as part of a building scheme, can be enforced by your fellow residents, and so cannot be disregarded.

Even if you escape from complying with official rules, but build something that is unsafe, you nevertheless have common-law liabilities towards third parties because of an act of negligence on your part. Lack of official approval for your improvements could also jeopardise the future sale of your home, since the standard enquiries made before contracts are exchanged always ask whether any alterations have been carried out, and, if so, whether the appropriate approval was obtained from your local authority.

Finally, do not forget that if your property is mortgaged you must notify your mortgage lender of your intentions where structural alterations and other major changes to the property are involved.

OTHER RULES AND REGULATIONS

Building and planning controls make by far the biggest impact on any home improvement project, but there are three other areas in which rules and regulations also come into play: work involving your plumbing, your wiring and your gas supply.

Water supply bye-laws

Local water supply companies have produced their own water bye-laws for many years, and have the statutory powers with which to enforce them on their customers. Those regulations in force today are based on the Model Water Bye-Laws drawn up in 1986 and, apart from some minor local variations, apply across the whole of the UK.

These bye-laws exist in order to prevent waste, undue consumption, contamination, or any other misuse of the water supply. They apply to any new work you may carry out on your plumbing system (and also on your heating system if it uses hot water to heat the radiators).

Under the bye-law requirements you must give your water supply company at least five working days' notice if you propose installing or altering (as opposed to repairing or replacing) a bidet, a flushing cistern, a tap to which a hose may be connected, or any fitting through which contamination of the water supply by back siphonage could occur (a bath fitted with shower mixer taps, for example). In Scotland you must give notice of installing or altering any water fitting.

Wiring Regulations

The Wiring Regulations, initially produced by the Institution of Electrical Engineers and now British Standard, do not have the force of law except in Scotland, where they form part of the Building Regulations. This means that elsewhere, anyone can carry out their own wiring work without having to comply with any rules. Electricity supply companies have the right to inspect and test any electrical work that they think may be unsafe, and they can also refuse to supply an unsafe installation, or one that does not satisfy the Wiring Regulations.

You should, for obvious reasons, make sure that any wiring work that you do in your home complies with the Wiring Regulations. If you are unsure of your ability to do this, always leave wiring work to a qualified electrician.

Gas Safety Regulations

Under the Gas Safety Regulations, it is illegal for anyone to carry out work on gas supply pipes, fittings and appliances unless they are competent enough to do so. This therefore means that you should leave all gas work to a qualified fitter.

Part 5

DECIDING WHO
SHOULD DO THE WORK

*Y*ou should now know exactly what sort of home improvements you want. For a complex or large-scale project you may have enlisted a professional adviser to help you realise your dreams. You have discovered whether official approval is needed for the work, you have applied for this if it is, and you have, one hopes, received it. It is now time to start getting more practical.

What you should do next is to look at the project you are planning in detail in order to decide whether it is wholly a do-it-yourself project, one that you would prefer to be carried out entirely by professionals, or one that needs some specialist input only at critical stages, perhaps with some do-it-yourself contributions at the appropriate points.

MAKING UP YOUR MIND

There are several factors you need to consider when making this decision. The first is your own level of skill: if you are competent and experienced in do-it-yourself work, you could, in theory, tackle anything, although there are many projects that you clearly could not manage single-handedly. You may feel that you are better at some skills than at others, and so decide to call in the specialists – a plumber, for example, or a plasterer – only when you need them. You may decide that you are best employed on the project just as a source of cheap labour, doing relatively unskilled parts of the work, such as site preparation or decoration at the end of the job. The choice is yours, but you need to make it now, since it will affect every other facet of the project.

The second key factor in making a decision is time. A project will be completed far more quickly if you hand it over to the professionals rather than tackling it yourself, so consider carefully whether this factor matters to you and your family. Living in chaos for months can tax the patience of a saint, so you should consider what your project involves in terms of the disruption to your daily existence. Building a conservatory, for example, will cause relatively few problems, since most of the work will be done outside the house, while carrying out a loft conversion, rewiring the house, or refitting the kitchen will be far more intrusive.

The third deciding factor is money. In principle, you will save money by doing the work yourself, since your labour will be unpaid. You will have the opportunity to shop around for keen prices for the building materials, and, by taking your time, you can spread the cost of the project to suit your budget. In practice, however, the saving may be marginal, since the professionals will be able to buy their materials at discounted trade prices, and their labour charges are generally extremely competitive. It therefore pays to compare the various options very carefully before making a decision about which one to choose (see Part 6 for more information about costing your project).

BREAKING DOWN THE JOB

To help you reach a decision about how much professional help you will need, break down the project that you are intending to tackle into separate stages, so that you can see which skills are required for each. The project checklists later in the book will help you to do this.

To illustrate how this process works, consider the building of a two-storey home extension – probably the biggest project you are ever likely to contemplate. The following are the main stages involved in its construction, and the skills that will be needed for each.

Site preparation

The site for the extension will have to be cleared, ready for the foundation trenches to be dug. This is hard and time-consuming manual labour, but will save you money if you do it yourself. If you prefer not to do so, hire an excavator and driver by the hour.

Foundations and over-site concrete

Placing and compacting large quantities of ready-mixed concrete is also hard physical work, and requires a team of helpers if you intend doing it yourself. Calling in a builder to do the job will add only about 25 per cent to the cost of the basic materials.

Underground drainage work

You will probably have to make alterations to the existing drainage arrangements for the disposal of surface water and foul water, involving laying new drain runs, constructing manholes, and perhaps digging a soakaway. This work is more labour-intensive than laying foundations, but is relatively inexpensive in terms of buying the materials. You might prefer to leave it to your builder if he is already carrying out your foundation work.

The extension's walls

Doing the brick- and blockwork for a two-storey extension is a far cry from building a garden wall, and you will need proper scaffolding throughout the duration of the job. The work also involves placing lintels over door and window openings, as well as building in floor joists, and door and window frames as the walls rise. By all means tackle the job if you are an experienced bricklayer, and can complete the work quickly so that the scaffolding hire charges do not mount up. Otherwise, employ a bricklayer and labourer; you can expect their labour to cost roughly as much as the price of the raw materials that they will be using.

The extension's roof

If you are giving your extension a pitched roof, marrying it to the existing house roof will involve some extensive and relatively complex work. Since this will include opening up the roof and exposing its structure to the weather, you will want the job completed as quickly as possible, so there is a good case for getting a professional roofer to do the work. His labour charges will typically be less than half the cost of the raw materials required.

Internal work

Once the extension's outer skin is complete, you will need a whole range of different skills. There will be windows to be glazed, initial plumbing and wiring work to be done, floorboards to be laid, walls to be plastered, ceilings to be fixed and skimmed, doors to be hung, and so on. Some building work will also be necessary to create access from the house to the extension. Get professional help as necessary if you feel that your carpentry, plumbing, electrical or plastering skills are not up to scratch.

Fitting and finishing

This is likely to be the area in which most people will feel able to do the work themselves, since it involves traditional do-it-yourself jobs such as connecting plumbing and electrical fittings, painting, paperhanging and laying floor coverings. All these tasks are relatively labour-intensive, so doing them yourself rather than leaving them to the professionals will offer considerable savings.

By stripping down any project to its bare bones like this you will be able to identify clearly the type of professional help you will need. You can then decide whether you want to employ one main contractor to run the whole project, whether to do everything yourself, or only some of the work, bringing in specialist sub-contractors as and when you need them.

FINDING THE PROFESSIONALS

Finding competent and reliable contractors to carry out home improvement work has never been easy. There follow some of the options you could explore.

Personal recommendation

The best way of finding a good contractor has always been by personal recommendation, since this imposes a burden of complete honesty on all parties. If someone has done satisfactory work for friends or relatives, you can get a first-hand account of the person's workmanship, time-keeping, cleanliness and general attitude. You will also get the opportunity to inspect the work personally. This method may not, however, be viable if you have just moved to a different area, although asking for advice can be a good way of breaking the ice with your new neighbours. Moreover, you may not get any leads by asking around; if no one has employed a good plumber lately, you will have to try another approach.

If you are employing a professional adviser such as an architect on your project, he or she may be able to recommend individual contractors. The advice should be completely impartial, but take up references anyway.

Spotting local talent

A recommendation need not come from someone you know: if you see work of the type you want being carried out locally, approach the householder and ask how the job is going. Most people are only too happy to talk about their own home improvement projects – unless, of course, they turned into disasters.

Many contractors put up a sign, or park their vans outside the house on which they are working, and will generally not mind being approached (although it is polite to make the initial contact through the householder). Alternatively, simply telephone the number displayed on the sign or van.

Telephone directories

Your local *Yellow Pages* phone directory will list contractors under individual trade headings, and you will find plenty to choose from. Some have display advertisements giving details of the sort of work they undertake, and these may also reveal whether the individual or firm is a member of a relevant trade association, or has the necessary professional qualifications (but see Trade associations and professional bodies, opposite, for a word of warning about false membership claims). Having a listing in a directory implies a certain level of permanence, although this does not guarantee performance standards.

The drawback to this method is that when you make contact, you are doing so 'cold', with little or no knowledge of whom you are calling. Start by asking whether they do the sort of work you require, and then ask them whether they would be prepared to put you in touch with satisfied customers in the area so that you can get a few references and also inspect their workmanship.

Local advertisements

You will also find contractors advertising in local newspapers and free sheets, and occasionally on newsagents' notice boards. This is often a good way of finding individuals to carry out specific tasks, as well as general builders, but once again the contact is cold. Individual contractors may be easier to contact in the evening or at weekends, although many of the more entrepreneurial types are never far from their mobile phones.

Cold-calling

You have probably already suffered from the approaches of telephone salesmen ringing out of the blue to ask whether you are interested in having your kitchen or bathroom refitted, your windows replaced, or a conservatory installed. By all means arrange a follow-up visit if you are interested in what they have to offer, but be prepared to stand your ground and make a deal on your own terms.

Trade associations and professional bodies

As mentioned earlier, many contractors in the home improvement sector belong to a trade organisation (and sometimes several), or are registered members of a professional body. These organisations can be a valuable source of local contacts; you can find a list of the main organisations at the back of this book. Apart from putting you in touch with their members, many also offer back-up services, such as a complaints and arbitration scheme.

If a firm or individual belongs to, or is registered with, such an organisation, it may be a good indication of their professionalism, since many of these bodies require evidence of several years' trading and satisfactory accounts before being granted membership.

Sadly, it has become increasingly common in recent years for unscrupulous contractors falsely to claim membership of trade bodies in order to enhance their image. If you plan to contact a contractor via an advertisement in which any such membership is claimed, check the validity of the claim with the organisation concerned first.

CHOOSING A CONTRACTOR

Distinguishing the good contractor from the indifferent one (or, indeed, the out-and-out rogue) is never easy. Here are some useful pointers as to whether the individual or firm you have contacted is likely to be competent and trustworthy. Unsatisfactory answers to any of these questions suggest that you might be wise to look elsewhere.

♦ When you first telephoned, did you get a clear and firm response to your inquiry? A positive 'yes' and the offer of an early appointment is a good sign. Indecision, or a promise to call back, is not.

♦ On arranging the first appointment, did the contractor arrive on time? Bad timekeeping at this stage is a sure warning of trouble ahead.

♦ Did the contractor arrive in a clean vehicle (a car, or a van) displaying his business details? Old, unmarked vans may speak volumes about their drivers.

♦ Did he appear interested in what you wanted doing? A good contractor should be ready with positive suggestions regarding alternative ways of doing the job, or different materials to use, while still leaving you to make the final decision.

♦ Did he offer, without prompting, to put you in touch with other satisfied customers? Be wary if he says he has just started work in the area.

♦ Did you like him as a person? If he is going to be around your house for a while, it will help enormously if you get on together.

Builders

You will probably want to call in a firm of builders for any large-scale projects in which you want minimal personal involvement, especially when a number of different trades are involved. Such firms will either directly employ the different craftsmen they require, or else will sub-contract the work to other firms as the need arises.

You can get the names of building firms in your area from the Federation of Master Builders*, the Building Employers Confederation*, or the Guild of Master Craftsmen* (see the list of addresses at the end of the book). The first two offer warranty schemes that guarantee materials and workmanship, and also completion of the work by another approved contractor if the firm you are using is unable to deliver for any reason.

Electricians

Electrical work is one area that many do-it-yourself enthusiasts prefer to leave to a professional. You may need an electrician either for a wholly electrical project, such as rewiring your house, or to carry out the electrical part of the work involved in another project.

You can get the names of qualified electricians from the National Inspection Council for Electrical Installation Contracting (NICEIC)*, the Electrical Contractors Association (ECA)*, and the Electrical Contractors Association of Scotland* (see the list of addresses at the end of this book for details). All three offer a complaints procedure and a completion-guarantee scheme.

Plumbers

Plumbing work is more popular among do-it-yourself devotees, but you may prefer to employ a professional for major projects, such as installing a central heating system, or plumbing in a new bathroom. Always employ a qualified fitter – someone who is either registered with the Council for Registered Gas Installers (CORGI)*, or who works for British Gas – if the work involves any work on your gas supply pipework.

You can get the names of registered plumbers from the Institute of Plumbing* (included in the list of addresses at the back of this book).

Most plumbers also tackle central heating work, and may be members of the National Association of Plumbing, Heating and Mechanical Services Contractors*, or of the Heating and Ventilating Contractors Association*.

Roofers

Roofing installation work is generally best left to the professionals because of the need to make the structure weatherproof as quickly as possible. There are also important safety aspects for the do-it-yourself roofer to consider, especially where working on pitched roofs is concerned.

You can get the names of registered roofers from the National Federation of Roofing Contractors*.

Package contractors

There is an ever-increasing number of firms in the home improvement market offering so-called 'package deals' for projects, including complete kitchen and bathroom refits, the replacement of windows, exterior wall treatments, conservatories and loft conversions. Such packages can seem attractive because the company takes care of everything, from the initial design through to the finished product. However, you usually pay a price for this aspect of convenience, and it is always wise to compare the price of the package deal with a more conventional approach to the project using local builders and contractors.

There are plenty of reputable firms with well-established businesses operating in this field. There are also numerous rogue operators, many of whom feature regularly in the consumer 'watchdog' horror stories of the press and television. As always, personal recommendation counts for a great deal, as can membership of a relevant trade organisation, such as the Federation of Master Builders*, or the Glass and Glazing Federation*. You can get lists of member firms and help with complaints in two individual product areas: the Kitchen Specialists Association* and the Conservatory Association*, respectively.

Part 6

WORKING OUT THE COST

*T*he next stage you have to tackle is one of the most important: working out how much your project is going to cost. For a wholly do-it-yourself job, work out precisely which materials you will need, and then shop around for the best prices you can find. If you are employing contractors, they will generally be responsible for buying all the basic materials required.

DOING THE WORK YOURSELF

Estimating the quantities of materials needed is relatively easy for some projects (installing a new central heating system, for example, or replacing a bathroom suite), since itemising everything is quite a straightforward process. It can be a much more difficult task for complex jobs involving a diverse range of products, and in this case you will save time, and avoid the problem of ordering too much or too little, by getting some professional help.

If you have employed an architect or surveyor to produce detailed plans for the work, he will be able (for an additional fee) to draw up a detailed specification of materials for you. You could also ask a builder or other contractor to do the same, although you will have to pay for this service, and you may have difficulty persuading the person to help if he is not going to be doing the work himself.

One area in which do-it-yourself enthusiasts find estimating quantities particularly difficult is masonry. As a rough guide, you need 60 bricks per square metre of wall laid in stretcher bond (like the outside leaf of a standard cavity wall), and 10 standard 450x225mm walling blocks per square metre for the inner leaf, and for internal partition walls. As far as the mortar is concerned, one 50kg bag of cement will make up about 0.25cu m of mortar, which is enough to lay about 800 bricks, or 375 walling blocks.

Collins Home Improvements Price Guide, which details both the cost of materials and the charges contractors are likely to make for a huge range of projects, is an invaluable aid to the do-it-yourself worker who is trying to estimate the cost of home improvement projects with some degree of accuracy. The guide also includes estimates of how long jobs will take, and gives each one a level of difficulty – essential advice when it comes to deciding whether to tackle a job yourself or to call in an expert.

WHERE TO SHOP

If you are familiar with your local do-it-yourself superstores and what they stock, by all means use them as a benchmark for estimating the cost of the materials and equipment needed for your project. However, they cannot compete on price (especially for large quantities) or product range with the sort of specialist outlets that contractors use; these are no longer the sole preserve of the contractor – many now go out of their way to gain the custom and trust of do-it-yourself customers as well.

Builders' merchants

Builders' merchants will be your first port of call for many of the projects described in this book. They are the obvious choice for buying bulk supplies of building materials of all types, and many deal in timber, plumbing, heating and electrical products, too. They will deliver materials on your behalf, and, if you are tackling a large project, they will open an account for you. It is worth asking for a trade discount: you could strike lucky. Their staff are generally extremely knowledgeable about the materials that they stock, and they can also be a very valuable source of free technical advice.

There is one important point to watch out for when using a builders' merchant to cost your project, however. Their displayed prices seldom include VAT (builders can claim it back, but you cannot), and finding that your total bill has to be increased by 17.5 per cent can come as a nasty shock when you already have a tightly costed budget.

Other specialist merchants

Depending on what your project involves, you may want to take your shopping list to other types of specialist outlets – timber merchants, plumbing or electrical wholesalers, kitchen or bathroom showrooms, and the like – in order to compare their prices with those offered by superstores and builders' merchants. Always make sure that you are comparing like with like.

Second-hand outlets

If you want to match existing features of your house, such as the brickwork, the roof tiles or the sash windows, it is worth finding out whether there are any architectural salvage firms in your area which carry stocks of reclaimed materials. You may well pay less than for new materials.

Hire shops

Apart from materials, for some of the more ambitious home improvement projects you are sure to need some additions to your do-it-yourself toolkit. You have two choices: to buy or to hire. Work out which extra tools and specialist equipment you will need for the job, and then decide how long you will need to hire them. Get price lists from local plant-hire firms. Buy anything that you expect to use regularly for the duration of the project, or which will cost more to hire for the time during which you will need it than to buy; you can always sell it at the end of the project if you will have no further need for it. Plan to hire tools needed for short periods only as and when you need them, but make sure that you order them well in advance so that you know that they will be available.

It is also worth considering buying or hiring professional versions of the power tools that you already own. They are built to withstand heavier and more prolonged use than tools designed for the do-it-yourself market, which can break down or burn out if overloaded.

Getting things home

Wherever possible, get materials and equipment delivered to your home by your supplier. You can, of course, use your car for transporting small quantities or delicate items, but you must not overload it. Two bags of cement weigh the same as two eight-stone passengers, and a hundred bricks weigh about a quarter of a ton, or as much as three twelve-stone people. A load of that weight in the boot can seriously impair the car's handling, so if you have to carry such materials, try to load the car evenly. Check the handbook for the maximum load that the car can carry, and do not exceed it.

If you are carrying things on a roof rack, make sure that they are well secured, and that any overhanging parts are clearly marked so that they attract the attention of other road-users. You must do this by law if anything projects by more than 1.8m (6ft) beyond the front of the car, or 1.07m (about 3ft 6in) beyond the back, and you must also have another person in the car if the front projection is more than 1.8m (6ft).

If you want to collect your materials yourself and prefer to protect your car from possible damage, hire a van or pick-up truck.

EMPLOYING CONTRACTORS

If you have decided to hand over your project (or part of it) to the experts, now is the time to get your chosen contractors more closely involved, by inviting them to give you a price for doing the work.

Inviting quotations

Assuming that you have already established their interest in the project, and perhaps had an initial site meeting with them, you should now write to the contractors asking them to give you a quotation for the work. Approach at least three contractors in order to ensure that you get the most competitive price, and make it clear to each that they are in competition for the contract. Do this well in advance of the time when you hope the work will start: good builders are usually booked up for months in advance.

If the project is relatively straightforward – fitting replacement windows, for example, or installing a new bathroom suite and tiling the room – the contractor may be able to price the job simply by making a site visit. For more complex jobs he will need further information: proper drawings as well as detailed specifications that include any particular products that you want used. Make sure that you have enough copies for each contractor.

When you ask for a quotation, tell the contractor when you want his response; it is usual to allow up to four weeks for this. Ask how long the quoted price will remain valid, and whether it includes VAT. The contractor must be registered for VAT if he is to add it to your bill, and with sizeable sums involved it pays to check his registration with your local VAT office; unscrupulous and unregistered firms have been known to add it to bills as an illegal way of making a further 17.5 per cent profit out of unsuspecting and gullible clients.

Assessing quotations

Study all the quotations carefully. You will mainly be interested in the price, and you may find that the difference between individual quotations is surprisingly wide. Do not assume that a very high quotation means that you will get a first-class job: it is usually the contractor's way of saying that he does not want the job, but he will do it if you are prepared to pay over the odds.

Be suspicious of an unusually low quotation. This may mean that the contractor will be using inferior materials, or will be subcontracting parts of the job to inexperienced and inexpensive workers. Without revealing the estimates given in the other quotations, ask him to justify his price, and check that he has fully understood the scope of the project. You should accept a very low quotation only if you are confident that you will get what you want for the price. You may, of course, get a bargain.

The amount of detail you receive will vary from firm to firm. The job should be broken down into individual stages (this breakdown is known as a schedule), and should clearly state where you have specified that particular materials or fittings are to be used. The schedule should also say who is responsible for supplying these items.

If you did not specify the individual items needed for the job – the bathroom suite, for example – the quotation will include them within what is known as a 'provisional sum'. This will be replaced in the final bill by the net cost of whatever the contractor fits, as well as a proportion of his overheads and profit charges. Where he will be employing specialist subcontractors for parts of the work, he should identify these parts, and should include a prime cost (pc) sum in the quotation, representing the subcontractor's own price for the work. Again, the main contractor will add his overheads and profit to this figure.

The quotation should also cover the following points.

♦ The person who is responsible for obtaining any necessary official permission before the work can get under way. If permission has already been obtained, the quotation should state that work will be carried out in accordance with the approved plans.

♦ The person responsible for insuring the work and materials while the contractor is working in your home. Professional contractors should have both employer's liability and public liability insurance; these cover them for damage to property, and for injuries to their employees and third parties.

♦ How any variations to the original specification, as far as materials, methods, timing or costs are concerned, will be agreed between the two parties. These should always be made in writing.

♦ When the work will start, and when it is likely to be completed.

♦ An itemised breakdown of the cost of the work, including VAT if appropriate, and details of how payments are to be made. Most contractors prefer some form of staged payment, especially on major projects. It is unwise to agree to pay upfront for materials: a reputable builder will have good credit with his suppliers, and will not have to pay for materials immediately.

♦ Details of any guarantees offered, especially if these are backed by insurance, or a trade organisation's indemnity scheme.

These details will eventually form part of the contract. Some firms include them on a separate standard form of contract sent with the quotation; others may print them on the back. Read them carefully, and discuss any terms you do not understand, or which seem to favour the contractor unfairly. It is too late to change them once you have signed the contract.

Making a decision

Other factors apart from the price may sway you in favour of a particular contractor. One may be able to start earlier than the others, or to complete the work more quickly. He may simply have made a good impression during your dealings with him, or may have done work of an impressively high standard for other customers which he has invited you to inspect. The choice is yours.

When you have made up your mind, and have clarified any points of disagreement over detail, write and accept the chosen quotation. It is courteous to notify the unsuccessful applicants at the same time.

SETTING REALISTIC TIMESCALES

If you are employing contractors to carry out your home improvement project, they will to all intents and purposes set the timescale for the project once you have agreed on a starting date for the work. Their experience in carrying out similar jobs will enable them to estimate with reasonable accuracy how long yours will take, and barring unforeseen snags they should finish within the agreed time.

If you are carrying out the project yourself, setting a timescale can be much more difficult; it depends largely on the scale of the work. You may be a competent enough plumber to be able to strip out your old bathroom fittings and install the new suite in a weekend, allowing the following two weekends in which to complete the fitting and finishing work. You may be able to take two weeks of your annual holiday to rewire the house or build your new conservatory.

Most do-it-yourself improvement projects, however, tend to have a definite starting point and a very vague completion date, because work has to be fitted in round day jobs and domestic commitments. If you can, break down the job into small stages, and allocate available work periods to each one. By doing this, you will have the satisfaction of seeing real progress as you tick off the passing of individual milestones, instead of helplessly feeling that you have a very high mountain to climb. Above all, be realistic in your estimates of how long a job will take, and be grateful that your labour comes free.

RAISING THE MONEY

How you decide to pay for your home improvement projects depends on your individual financial situation. For most people, the choice lies between spending savings or borrowing the money. If you have sufficient savings to pay for the work, you have to take into account the loss of the unearned income that has resulted from spending the deposit. You may also be unwilling to dissipate a nest egg set aside for a rainy day. Only you can decide whether to spend it, or whether to save it and borrow what you need for the project.

Borrowing the money is potentially much more complicated, since there are so many sources for loans. For relatively inexpensive projects – costing up to, say, £5,000 – a personal loan from a bank or building society, repayable over a period of up to five years, is probably the preferred option. For more expensive improvements, the best way of keeping repayments down to a manageable level is to approach your mortgage lender and ask for an increase in your mortgage. Since your lender already holds your home as security for the loan, your request should readily be agreed to unless you are close to a negative equity position.

Whichever borrowing route you take, evaluate your financial circumstances carefully to make sure that you can afford the repayments, especially if the house is held as security. There is little point in embarking on an expensive project if it ends up bankrupting you.

Local authority grants

Grants are available from your local authority to help pay for the cost of certain types of home improvement work. However, there is far less money available nowadays for this type of funding than used to be the case, and fund allocation is at the discretion of the local authority, except in certain cases. Tax relief on loans used for home improvement work was withdrawn in April 1988, following widespread abuse of the rules.

♦ *Renovation grants* are mandatory, not discretionary, and are intended for bringing old properties up to modern standards. This means ensuring that the house is structurally sound, is weatherproof, and has certain basic amenities. You have to live in the house for at least a year after obtaining this grant.

♦ *Discretionary renovation grants* may be available for other work, such as thermal insulation and central heating.

♦ *Grants for facilities for people with disabilities* are also mandatory, and are used to meet the needs of an occupant who has a disability, or of a householder looking after a person with a disability in his or her home.

♦ *Common parts grants* are available to tenants living in flats to be put towards the cost of carrying out repair work to the common areas of the building, such as the roof, stairs and entrance hall. They are discretionary unless the landlord has been served with a repair notice.

♦ *Minor works grants* are intended to cover the cost of minor but essential works, and are available only to home owners and private sector tenants who receive income-related benefits.

The best way of finding out whether you are eligible for grant aid is to contact your local authority or a Citizens Advice Bureau. Even if you are successful in obtaining a grant, the actual amount you will receive will depend on the outcome of a financial circumstances test.

Part 7

Drawing up Contracts

*I*t always pays to put things in writing before you employ an outside contractor. Even the simplest contract document will give both parties a clear indication of what the job involves and how it is to be carried out, and will help to avoid confusion as the work progresses. Most importantly, it will give you (and the contractor) the protection of the law if its terms are breached by either party.

LETTERS OF AGREEMENT

For small-scale improvements you may need only a simple letter of agreement, signed by both parties. This should cover the following points:

♦ a brief description of the job to be done
♦ the agreed price for the work (with a copy of the contractor's original quotation attached to the back of the letter)
♦ the person responsible for obtaining any necessary official approval for the work
♦ the agreed starting and finishing dates; the phrase 'time is of the essence' should be included if meeting the latter is important
♦ how you will pay for the work, and, if you have agreed to make staged payments, when they will fall due
♦ whether any part of the payment can be withheld in the event of a dispute arising between the parties, or on completion of the job, as a retainer against the cost of rectifying any defects found in the work.

QUOTATIONS AS CONTRACTS

Some contractors will supply quotations that are detailed enough to act as contracts, which may have the contractor's standard terms and conditions printed on the back of the quotation. These are especially common among firms offering package deals on home improvements such as conservatories, kitchen refits and replacement windows. Always read the terms carefully before you sign: they are often more for the supplier's benefit than yours, and once you have signed the document you are bound by them.

The major exception to this involves contracts for products such as replacement windows and new kitchens that are ordered in very specific circumstances. If the seller calls at your home without invitation, or visits you by appointment after making an unsolicited telephone call, and you then place an order for goods during that visit, you have some rights of cancellation, even if you have signed a contract. These are as follows:

♦ written notice of these rights must be given to you when you sign the order; if it is not, the seller cannot enforce the contract
♦ you then have a 'cooling-off' period of seven days, within which you can cancel the order by writing to the seller. Any deposit that you paid when you signed the order must be returned to you in full.

According to the provisions of the Consumer Credit Act 1974, you may also be able to cancel a signed contract if you agree to take credit to pay for the work. If the seller offers you credit directly, or acts as a broker by arranging credit for you with a professional lender, you can generally cancel the contract if all the following points apply:

♦ the amount of credit involved is between £50 and £15,000
♦ your house is not used as security for the loan
♦ you signed the credit agreement after discussing it face to face with the seller
♦ you signed it somewhere other (usually in your own home) than at the seller's or lender's premises.

You will be given a copy of the credit agreement when you sign it, and you should receive a second copy by post a few days later. These must both set out your rights of cancellation. You then have five days in which to decide whether you want to cancel the contract, starting from the date on which you received the second copy. Cancel the contract in writing, sending your letter to the seller by recorded delivery so that you have proof that it has been sent and received.

STANDARD CONTRACTS

If you are employing an architect to design and supervise your home improvement project, they will draw up the contract with your chosen contractor. This will probably be a Joint Contracts Tribunal (JCT) Minor Works contract. You can also use this form (which is available from the Royal Institute of British Architects*) if you are issuing the contract yourself; the contractor receives one copy and you keep the other.

    You may prefer to tailor a contract to suit the work that you are having carried out. It should ideally include all the following clauses (square brackets indicate the specific financial or other details which you need to insert).

Specimen contract

1. *[The contractor's name]* will carry out and complete the work outlined in the attached specification and drawings in a good and workmanlike manner, in accordance with all relevant British standards and codes of practice, to the reasonable satisfaction of *[the owner]*, all for the sum of *[the agreed price]*, plus VAT *[if applicable]* at the standard rate.

2. The contractor will provide all the materials, equipment, plant and labour necessary to carry out and complete the work.

3. The contractor will begin work on *[the starting date]*, will proceed regularly with the work, and will complete it by *[the finishing date]*, subject only to any changes agreed according to Clause 6. Time is of the essence with regard to this work.

4. Should the contractor fail to finish the work on time without good reason, he agrees to pay the owner damages, which represent the actual loss to the owner of *[an agreed figure]* for every week or part of a week during which completion is delayed.

5. The contractor will, within 14 days of completing the work, remove all tools, surplus materials and rubbish from the site, leaving it in a clean and tidy condition.

6. Any variation to the work, together with its cost and its effect on the original completion date, will be agreed in writing by both parties before the variation is carried out. Otherwise the completion date will be postponed only if the contractor is prevented from completing the job by factors outside his control.

7. The contractor will comply with all statutory requirements, local and national regulations and bye-laws that relate to the work, and will be responsible for making all the required notifications and arranging all necessary site inspections.

8. The contractor will take out appropriate employer's liability insurance and third party liability insurance to cover the work.

9. The contractor will make good at his own expense any damage to the owner's premises caused by him, his employees or his subcontractors.

10. If the contractor's work is not of a reasonable standard, or if the contractor leaves the site without reasonable explanation for more than *[an agreed number]* consecutive days, the owner may terminate the contract, paying only for the value of the work done, less compensation for inconvenience or any additional expenses incurred as a result.

11. The contractor will promptly, and at his expense, make good any defects resulting from materials or workmanship which are not in accordance with

the terms of the contract.

12. The owner will pay to the contractor *[an agreed figure, usually 90 or 95 per cent]* of the sum mentioned in Clause 1, or any other such sum as may be agreed in accordance with Clause 6, on submission of the contractor's final account following satisfactory completion of the work. The balance will be paid *[an agreed time]* from the date of completion, or when all defects arising have been made good in accordance with Clause 11, whichever is the later.

(12a – an alternative to Clause 12 for long projects.)

The owner will make interim payments of *[the agreed amounts]* to the contractor on satisfactory completion of the following stages of the work *[list the stages]*.

13. The owner and the contractor agree that, should any dispute between them arise, either party will give the other written notice of the dispute. If this cannot be resolved by discussion and negotiation, they will refer the matter to an arbitrator agreed by both parties, whose decision will be final and binding.

Here is a brief explanation of what the individual clauses mean.

Clause 1 sets the overall price for the work, and may refer to additional 'prime cost' sums for work to be carried out by specialist subcontractors. It allows you to claim damages if the work is not carried out to the specified standards.

Clause 2 may require some variation if, for example, you are providing any specific materials yourself.

Clause 3 makes it clear that compliance with the agreed starting and completion dates is a vital part of the contract, and allows you to invoke clauses 4 and 6 if necessary. However, you must be prepared for unavoidable delays due, for example, to illness, bad weather, or hold-ups in the supply of materials because of manufacturing difficulties, all of which are beyond the contractor's control.

Clause 4 ensures that you are compensated for any small, acceptable overruns that are the contractor's fault. The figure, which you should agree in advance and insert into the contract, is not a penalty, but is intended to pay for your inconvenience, and to cover any additional costs that you may incur as a result of the overrun.

Clause 5 puts the onus on the contractor not to leave unwanted materials, plant or rubbish on the site once the work is completed. You could add a statement to the effect that the final bill will not be paid until this clause has been satisfied.

Clause 6 aims to protect both parties if either wants to make any changes to the specification after work has started. Once any changes have been agreed, and their effect on costs and timing have been assessed, make a note of them in duplicate. Both parties should sign each copy and retain one.

Clause 7 ensures that the contractor is responsible for complying with the requirements of the planning authorities, the local building control department, and any other laws or bye-laws. If you yourself have applied for, and received, planning permission and/or Building Regulations approval, it can be varied as necessary to cover only notifications and inspections.

Clause 8 is essential, even if your own household insurance covers such eventualities as an injury to a member of the public. You should ask to see evidence that the contractor's insurance cover exists.

Clause 9 is effectively another insurance clause for your protection. Check the

site every day for damage, and inform the contractor immediately if any occurs. Keep written records of when the original damage occurred, and what action (if any) was taken to rectify it.

Clause 10 is your ultimate weapon against a recalcitrant contractor, but should not be used without good cause and due notice. It is wise to get legal advice before invoking it.

Clause 11 guarantees the work once it has been completed. (See also **Guarantee schemes**, below, for more information.)

Clause 12 and 12a detail how you will pay the contractor. Retaining a small percentage of the total is a guarantee of sorts that the contractor will put right any defects which may only show up after completion. Staged payments may be unavoidable for large projects, but you should avoid paying any money for materials before the work starts. If the contractor's credit rating with his suppliers of materials is not good, it is a poor sign of his general status.

Clause 13 is worth including for complex projects where unforeseen difficulties could arise which might need professional resolution. (See **Dealing with disputes**, overleaf, for more information.)

A contract containing these terms should cover every reasonable eventuality, and will not penalise an honest and hard-working contractor. After you have discussed and agreed the details, each party should sign two copies and retain one.

GUARANTEE SCHEMES

The biggest fear of many home-owners, as far as major home improvement projects are concerned, is the risk of the contractor going out of business, either before completing the work, or soon afterwards, thus making any guarantees he may have offered worthless unless they are insurance-backed.

There are a number of building industry guarantee schemes which may be worth joining if you are planning a long and involved project, or one in which a delay would constitute a serious problem. One of these is the Building Guarantee Scheme, incorporated as an option in the JCT Minor Works contract mentioned earlier. This offers cover for disputes regarding the quality of the work, as well as for the insolvency of the contractor, for a period of 30 months after the completion of the job, and is available for any home improvement project costing between £500 and £100,000.

The Independent Warranty Association* scheme covers the installation of replacement windows, conservatories, kitchens and bathrooms, and will give protection in the event of a contractor going out of business. It ensures that any uncompleted work is finished, and also that any necessary remedial work is done.

The Guarantee Protection Trust* scheme is restricted to projects involving the treatment of damp, woodworm and rot, and so has limited relevance to most home improvement projects.

You may find that you are covered for the completion of unfinished work if the contractor concerned is a member of a trade association, but you generally need to notify the association before work starts in order to be accepted for cover.

If the work you are having carried out is covered by one of the guarantee schemes mentioned above, include their details in the contract.

Paying on credit

If you arrange for a loan to pay for all, or part of, the work with the contractor, or if you pay a deposit using your credit card, the finance or credit company is

jointly liable with the contractor for any problems that occur subsequently. If the contractor goes out of business, or otherwise breaks your contract, you can claim therefore against the credit company concerned. Under the terms of the Consumer Credit Act 1974, this protection is available for loans to buy specific goods or services where the lender has a contract with the supplier, and applies if the cash value of the work or goods is between £100 and £30,000, and the loan is for less than £15,000. It is not available for general bank loans.

DEALING WITH DISPUTES

The terms of your contract are intended to eliminate the likelihood of a dispute arising as work proceeds on your project. However, things can still go wrong, and prompt and effective action is the best way of remedying the situation.

Start by discussing the problem. If this does not resolve matters, put your complaint in writing and send it to the contractor, specifying what you want done, and giving him a deadline in which to comply. Keep copies of all relevant notes and correspondence, as well as a diary of events.

Get an independent expert to back up your complaint. This could be another contractor, an architect or surveyor, or a member of a relevant trade association. You may have to pay for the advice, but it could be worth doing if you end up taking legal action over the dispute. Trade associations may offer a conciliation service, which is free if your contractor is a member of the association.

If you are sure that the contractor is in breach of the contract, consider withholding any further payment until the dispute is resolved. If you have a credit agreement, however, it is worth getting legal advice on your position, as you may run into problems if you fall behind with your payments. As mentioned under **Guarantee schemes**, above, the existence of a credit agreement makes the lender jointly liable if the contractor defaults, so you should inform your lender of the dispute at the earliest opportunity.

If the dispute remains unresolved, you have two further courses of action. The first is to go to arbitration; you may have already agreed to this in your contract (Clause 13), or it may be suggested by an involved trade association. The second is to take your contractor to court.

Disputes can only go to arbitration if both sides agree to this. You should request arbitration from the Chartered Institute of Arbitrators*; each side then submits its case in writing only. The arbitrator studies the evidence submitted, and then notifies both parties of his decision, which is both legally binding and legally enforceable.

If you decide to go to court, and the amount at issue is less than £1,000 (£750 in Scotland), you can use the so-called 'small claims' procedure. You will get advice from your local Citizens Advice Bureau on how to proceed with the case. For larger amounts, consult a solicitor before proceeding, since your claim will be dealt with in the county court rather than by a district judge.

Part 8

LIVING WITH THE JOB

*A*ll home improvement work is disruptive. The degree to which it will interfere with your everyday life depends on the scale of the project, on whether you are doing it yourself or employing outside contractors, and on whether the project is being professionally supervised or not. In an ideal world, you would employ an architect or surveyor to manage the entire project, and then go away on holiday until it was finished. In the real world, however, you will simply have to live through it.

The secret of making life bearable during the upheaval lies in having a complete understanding of what the job will involve, and in making thorough preparations before work starts. You should have acquired the former knowledge as you progressed through the various planning stages, and the checklists for specific projects given later in the book provide further details. As for making the preparations, here are some suggestions. Not all will apply to every project, but by checking them off one by one you will be able to decide which are relevant to you.

BEFORE WORK STARTS

One of the most important steps to take before work starts is to inform your neighbours of what you are planning to do. They will already have been notified by your local authority about any large-scale projects requiring planning permission, but even if they have no objections in principle to the work being carried out, they may well react with horror once it starts. If you have them on your side from the beginning, life will be much easier for all parties. Sort out the following issues in particular.

♦ In semi-detached or terraced properties, work may affect party walls. Before work starts, carry out an inspection of both sides of the wall (which will obviously require your neighbour's consent), and make written notes as to its condition, which both parties should then sign and date.

♦ You or your contractors may need access from your neighbour's property, for example, in order to erect or dismantle scaffolding. You cannot proceed without his or her permission, so make sure that this is forthcoming, ideally in the form of a letter.

♦ Dust, and possibly larger pieces of debris, will inevitably fall on your neighbour's property as the work proceeds. Tell your neighbour that you will clean his or her windows, wash down paintwork, sweep paths, and so on, whenever necessary, and that your contractor is insured for any damage that he might cause to the property or to any vehicles parked on it.

♦ Building work is bound to be noisy. Try to agree with your neighbour the times when particularly noisy work will cause the least disruption.

As far as your own preparations are concerned, here are some possible courses of action to consider.

♦ In areas of the house which are likely to be affected by the work, pack away all breakable items, and buy or hire dustsheets with which to cover your furniture and floor coverings (or remove them completely from the area if this is preferable and you have storage space available).

♦ Consider sending children or elderly relatives to stay with family or friends for the duration of the project if major disruption to the house and its services is anticipated. Arrange for your pets to go to boarding kennels, or to be looked after by neighbours or friends.

♦ Work out where you are going to store the materials for the project (whether in the open or under cover), and make sure that you have enough space available. It may be worth considering parking your car off the property, and well out of possible harm's way.

For a DIY project, make sure that you have all the tools and equipment you will need, or that you can hire it when required.

DOING THE WORK YOURSELF

You will obviously have full control (in theory at least) over how the work proceeds if you are doing it yourself, but you need to be aware that a DIY project always takes longer than you initially planned. This is because you will not be able to work continuously on it, unlike a contractor, and there will always be unforeseen diversions and delays that may have nothing to do with the job in hand. As the work proceeds, you will have to be meticulous about clearing the decks as far is as possible at the end of each session if you are to avoid turning the whole house into a building site. Above all, try to keep children away from the work site for safety's sake.

EMPLOYING CONTRACTORS

If you are employing contractors, you have every right to set the terms under which they will work in your home. You clearly cannot expect them to change into carpet slippers every time they cross the threshold, but you should make the ground rules clear from the start.

Begin by deciding on their best access route into, or through, the house. Remove as much furniture as possible from this path, and ask your contractor to put down taped or stapled dustsheets along the whole route, so that they will not get scuffed up in use. It is a wise precaution to request them to lay heavy-duty plastic runners, so that wet or muddy boots do not mark your floor coverings through the dustsheets. It may also be worth taping protective packing material to any door frames through which tools and materials will have to pass. Insist that internal doors are kept shut whenever possible to prevent dust spreading right through the house.

Work out which facilities the workmen may use, especially during lunch and tea breaks. You may be prepared to let them into your kitchen, or you may prefer to set up an old table and chairs in the garage or garden shed for their use; they may even prefer to take breaks in their van. If you are providing the catering facilities, make sure that they have access to the water supply and a kettle. Look out some cheap mugs, spoons and a tin tray, and leave tea, coffee, milk and sugar visible, so that they do not have to search the kitchen for these items. Provide ashtrays if they smoke, but make it clear if you do not want smoking inside. If you have a downstairs cloakroom, allocate that for their use, put down dustsheets, and provide a good supply of old towels. Otherwise, unless you are prepared to let them use the family bathroom, it may be preferable to hire a chemical toilet and site it in the garage or garden shed for the duration of the project. Decide whether to allow them the use of your telephone; many contractors now have mobile phones, but may still expect to make outgoing calls at your expense. You can have such calls barred at the telephone exchange if you will be away from the house during the progress of the work.

Make sure that deliveries to the site will not cause an obstruction, especially if they are to be left in the road. You need permission from your local authority highways department to do this, and also to park a skip in the road. Establish in advance who will be responsible for obtaining the necessary permits. Remember that any such obstructions in the road must be properly lit at night. Keep skips covered with a tied-on tarpaulin in order to stop other people dumping things in it. If piles of materials are to be left out in the open, make sure that they are put out of sight and well away from the road, so that unscrupulous passers-by are not tempted to help themselves.

Find out whether the contractors expect to leave their tools and equipment on the site at the end of the day. You could offer to store larger items in your garage or shed, but you may prefer to ask them to take their tools home with them. Make sure that any ladders are not a security risk, and that any windows that are accessible from ladders or scaffolding are secure.

If you will be at work or away while the job is being carried out, appoint one of the contractors 'head of security' and issue him with a set of keys. Make sure he knows how to lock up (and how to set and disarm the burglar alarm if you have one). Remove valuables from open display as a precautionary measure.

Ask for paths and other access areas to be swept at the end of each working day in order to minimise the transfer of sand, cement and mud into the house. Make sure that boarded runways are laid across lawns and flower beds to protect them from wheelbarrow tyres, and that special care is taken not to damage plants

and shrubs. Insist that the contractor's vehicles are parked in the road rather than on your driveway, for spillages of oil and other materials could make a permanent mess.

While the job is under way, your main priority is to ensure that all the work is being carried out according to the specification and the contract. Do not get too involved in the day-to-day running of the project: you will only get in the way and annoy the workmen, who generally hate being watched while they ply their trade. Intervene immediately only if you see something that is in obvious breach of the contract, and raise the subject tactfully rather than losing your temper. Otherwise, simply check the progress made each evening, and, if you find anything amiss, either telephone the contractor there and then, or leave written instructions for him to read the next morning. On long-running projects it is a good idea to suggest a regular meeting – say once a week – at which progress can be discussed and any problems ironed out. If you are not at home during the day, make sure that you leave details of where you can be contacted if necessary.

If you are employing an architect or surveyor to supervise the project for you, he will visit the site at regular intervals, and will handle all the necessary communication with the contractors. This need not prevent you from taking an interest in how the work is progressing, but remember that you should pass any comments or complaints you may have to your supervisor, rather than making them directly to the contractors.

INSPECTING THE FINISHED JOB

Once the work is finished, you should inspect it carefully to ensure that it meets the specification, and is of the standard that you expected. Leave this to your architect or surveyor if you employed one to supervise the project. Otherwise, go round the finished project carefully on your own before organising a meeting with your contractor to discuss any snags: defects or omissions that must be put right before the contract can be considered to have been completed satisfactorily.

Start by checking that the finished job conforms to the original specification, and do it section by section. Any major deviations from the specification should have come to light long ago, but there may be minor variations in fittings or finishes which were introduced only in the closing stages of the work.

Outside the house, inspect the exterior of the work closely, paying particular attention to details that could affect its weather resistance: things like pointing, flashings and mastic seals. Climb a ladder, or use binoculars, to take a closer look at work done at first-floor level. Make sure that the site is clean and tidy.

Indoors, check any new ceiling, and also the wall and floor surfaces and finishes, looking at them from various angles to ensure that they are true, sound, smooth and clean, especially if they have finished decorative features.

Similarly, check all new woodwork. Make sure that any glass panes in windows and doors are properly installed and secured, and that none is cracked. Open and close all new doors and windows to ensure that they move smoothly and without binding, and check that locks and fittings operate easily. Open and close new cupboard doors and drawers, and check their alignment in runs of units in kitchens and bedrooms.

Look at new plumbing work closely. Inspect supply pipework for leaks or weeping joints. Fill new appliances with water until they overflow to ensure that the overflow pipe works properly and does not leak. Empty the appliances, and then check that the traps and waste pipes are watertight. Flush the WC and check for leaks, then look inside the cistern to see if it is refilling correctly. Finally, look for evidence that any exposed metalwork has been correctly earthed: you should find special clamps and earth cables in place.

Check that new light switches, socket outlets and other electrical accessories work. Test the operation of any new protective devices fitted in the fuse box; there may be miniature circuit breakers in place of circuit fuses, and a residual current device to protect vulnerable circuits.

Switch on the central heating system, and check that the water heats up, that radiators warm up quickly and evenly, and that thermostats and other controls operate correctly. Listen for any unusual noises emanating from the system.

Note down in duplicate any defects or omissions you may find, and then arrange an on-site meeting with your contractor, and go through the list item by item. Give the contractor a copy of the list, and agree a reasonable time span within which things must be put right.

Finally, be reasonable when it comes to paying the final account. Do not withhold payment if the contract has been completed to all intents and purposes (so-called 'practical' completion). If you have a contract that stipulates the retention of a small percentage of the overall cost pending the correction of omissions or defects, add to that the actual cost of supplying any missing items or rectifying any faults, in case the contractor does not return to attend to them, and pay the outstanding balance. Contractors have bills to pay too.

HOME IMPROVEMENT PROJECTS

*T*his section looks at 30 of the most popular home improvement projects. In each case you will find details of the various options available, an outline of what the job will involve and information on the likely order of work, plus a summary of any Building Regulations and planning requirements the project may require. You can then decide what you intend to achieve and whether you want to do the work yourself or enlist the service of professionals.

Adaptations for people with disabilities

If you or someone in your family has a disability or uses a wheelchair, some careful planning is essential in order to create a manageable and comfortable home environment. Even some simple modifications and home improvements can make the house much less of an obstacle course. You may be able to get a grant from your local authority towards the cost of carrying out the work.

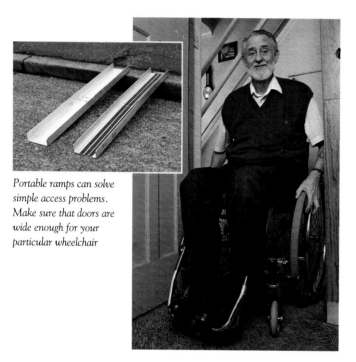

Portable ramps can solve simple access problems. Make sure that doors are wide enough for your particular wheelchair

OPTIONS

Getting in and out of the house

One of the most common complaints from disabled people is that they are effectively trapped in their own homes by access arrangements that present no problem for able-bodied people. The biggest obstacle for many, and in particular for users of wheelchairs and walking aids, are steps at the front door.

Tailor-made ramps are one solution to this problem, made either from timber or, for a more permanent installation, concrete. You can also buy a wide range of portable ramps, including folding, telescopic or wheeled ramps, some with side rails. Any ramp must be reasonably shallow so that it can be climbed

without undue effort, and descended in comparative safety. The recommended maximum gradient is about 1:10 over a distance of 5 metres or less, so a step that is 150mm (6in) high should be approached by a ramp that is 1.5m (5ft) long. If possible, the ramp should run straight up to the door, but if this is not feasible, it can run parallel to the wall, as long as a landing area about 1.2m2 (4sq ft) is provided in front of the door itself to allow a wheelchair to be turned easily. There must be a kerb of 100mm (4in) in height along any open side to keep the chair on course, and the ramp should be at least 1 metre wide. Add sturdy handrails at each side of the ramp for the convenience and safety of those using it on foot. Finally, make sure that the surface of a permanent ramp provides a good grip. Concrete ramps should therefore be given a lightly ribbed surface texture, and strips of non-slip material, such as roofing felt, should be stuck to timber ramps.

If the disabled person is able to use the steps, make sure that they are in good condition, and that they have a non-slip surface that drains water away freely, so that neither water nor ice makes the surface slippery. Add a sturdy handrail at each side of the flight of steps, extending it by about 300mm (12in) at each end to provide extra support.

Make sure that paths, steps and ramps are well lit at night, ideally by means of a two-way switching arrangement that can be operated by the user. An ideal solution is to use waterproof switches that are operated by a special key, and to site one at the entrance to the property – on a wall or gatepost, for instance – and the other next to the front door. Set them at a height that is easy to reach.

Check that the threshold itself does not present any obstacle, and add a shallow ramp in the hall if the threshold is slightly raised. Fit scuff plates to doors and door frames, and reposition handles and locks so that they are easier to reach. Lever handles are easier for people with stiff hands or poor grip.

Getting around the house

Moving around indoors can also be difficult for people with disabilities. The modifications that you will need to carry out will depend on the nature and degree of the person's disability, but the following points are some useful general guidelines.

♦ Ensure that all main traffic routes are clear of obstructions by rearranging or even removing furniture. Corridors should be 90cm wide to accommodate a wheelchair comfortably. Make sure that there is room for easy access to storage spaces, such as shelves, cupboards and built-in units.

♦ Door openings should be at least 75cm wide; most will allow a standard wheelchair to pass through them, but will need enlarging in the case of larger electric models. Check that there is enough room behind the door to allow it to be fully opened. It may be worth rehanging bathroom and WC doors so that they open outwards and thus give more room for manoeuvring within the room itself.

♦ Check that all floor coverings are fixed securely in place (also important for other people, especially if they are unsteady on their feet). As a rule, smooth floor coverings are much easier for manoeuvring wheelchairs than thick-pile carpets, which will also tend to wear unevenly along heavily used traffic routes around the house.

♦ If the person can walk, fit grab rails on the walls along traffic routes, and position strategically sited furniture to lean on and seats at convenient intervals to provide resting places.

Using the stairs

Stairs can be a major obstacle, even if the person can walk, and are a total barrier for those in wheelchairs. In the former case, it is essential that there is a sturdy handrail at each side of the flight of stairs, ideally of an open type that can be easily gripped. Make sure that the existing balustrade is secure; it needs to be strong enough to hold someone stumbling or falling against it. If the flight of stairs is situated against a wall, or rises between two walls, add a second rail fixed on wall brackets on the other side. Check that stair carpets are securely fitted, and avoid rugs altogether in the hall and on the landing. Also make sure that the stairwell lighting has two-way switching and that the switches are within easy reach.

For wheelchair users and people with severe disabilities who live in two-storey homes, there are two alternatives. One is to convert a ground-floor room into a bedroom, ideally complete with washing and WC facilities, unless these exist elsewhere on the

There are many adaptations and gadgets designed to make life easier for disabled people

same floor. The other option is to install a stairlift or, if space and funds permit, what is called a through-floor lift. Both are comparatively expensive.

Various types of stairlift are available. Some have a small platform on which the person can stand, while others include a chair that folds up when not in use. Larger models will take a wheelchair on a specially built, large platform. Stairlifts can be fitted to most staircase layouts, although they are expensive to install on stairs which are curved or have split flights. Fitting one is not a do-it-yourself job, however; get advice from an occupational therapist or a reputable supplier on the best type of stairlift for your particular requirements, and make sure that the equipment meets the requirements of British Standard BS5776.

For wheelchair users, through-floor lifts are an alternative to stairlifts, and installing one, although expensive, may cost less than moving house. They take up a lot of room on both floors, however, since there must be enough space to allow the user with a wheelchair or walking aid to enter and leave it easily. Again, seek professional advice if this seems the ideal solution to your requirements.

Improving the kitchen

The kitchen is, in many ways, the nerve centre of the house, and it is essential that disabled people have easy access to all its facilities. Making this possible is likely to involve some wholesale alterations to the room's fixtures and fittings, particularly if the person uses a wheelchair or lives alone.

Providing easy access to the kitchen units is one of the biggest challenges. Deep base units and tall wall cupboards can both become relatively inaccessible, but you can solve the problem by fitting pull-out drawers and corner carousels in base units, and installing spring-loaded, pull-down baskets in wall cupboards. Base units can also be fitted with a range of useful aids, from pull-out worktops to foldaway ironing boards, which can be installed at the perfect height for a wheelchair user. Pull-out mobile trolleys also provide an easy way of moving heavy things around the kitchen.

A kitchen that is dedicated to a wheelchair user will need worktops at a lower level than is usual – generally set around 800mm (32in) above floor level – with a space of no more than 375mm (about 15in) between the worktop and the underside of any wall units. In a shared kitchen, fit worktops at different heights. There are adjustable-height units but they

are generally very expensive to buy.

The sink poses its own particular problems. Yo may need to fit taps with easy-turn, lever-arm cor trols for people with weak hands, or, for wheelcha users, to move the taps to the front face of the sin unit. The sink will be easier to use if the wheelcha can be wheeled beneath it, and it will be easier still a height-adjustable sink with flexible plumbing an waste connection is fitted.

Cooking facilities need very careful planning. / separate hob and oven is ideal, with wheelcha access provided beneath the hob. A one-piec ceramic hob is easier to use (and to clean) than ind vidual hotplates or rings. For all users, a built-in ove at waist level will be better than one placed belo worktop level; one with a side-opening door is be for users in wheelchairs; while one with a drop-dow door that can thus provide a shelf on which to pu hot containers will suit people with weak hand: Have work surfaces at either side of the hob for mov ing pans to and from the hob.

As far as other appliances are concerned, choos front-loading washing machines and dish-washer with doors that are not too low or fit models that ca be installed at worktop level.

Finally, relocate light switches and socket outlet as necessary to make them easily accessible – at thigl or waist level, rather than ankle level – and fit plug with handles on portable appliances.

Improving the bathroom

The problems that bathrooms can pose for disable people revolve around the ease of access to the roor itself, and also the ease of use of its facilities. You ca often improve the former for wheelchair users b simply reversing the door to the room so that i opens outwards.

Taps with lever handles are ideal for those with a weak grip

The changes needed in order to make the room more user-friendly depend on the extent of the user's disabilities. You may need to do little more than ensure that the floor is made of non-slip material, that tap handles are of the easy-turn type, and that there are strong grab rails fitted alongside the bath, WC and wash basin, as well as within the shower cubicle. Furthermore, a raised toilet seat can make the WC easier to use, and is very simple to fit.

Using the bath can be awkward, even for people with slight disabilities. Fitting a short 'sitz' bath in place of the standard type may make getting in and out easier, while for people with more severe disabilities, some form of manual or powered bathlift will be essential. These are basically padded chairs which are level with the edge of the bath when raised, and which thus allow the user to sit down easily and swing the legs round into the bath; the chair is then lowered into the water so that the user can bathe in comfort without assistance.

Special shower cubicles are available for people with disabilities, featuring fold-down seats and ramps for easy wheelchair access. Some cubicles also contain a WC fitted with a waste macerator unit, so allowing you to provide essential facilities within a small floor area, such as in a room that is some way away from the existing drainage system. Another special type of WC incorporates a bidet and warm-air drying facility.

GETTING HELP

There are several agencies and organisations that can provide advice and help if you are modifying your home to suit the requirements of a disabled person. These include:

◆ your local authority's social services department (social work department in Scotland, health and social services board in Northern Ireland)

◆ home improvement agencies – there are about 250 such groups across the UK – usually called Care & Repair or Staying Put schemes. They can tell you about Handyperson services in some areas, which are often run by housing associations and have people who will carry out small DIY jobs

◆ the Disabled Living Foundation*, and the various centres that cater specifically for people with disabilities around the country

◆ voluntary agencies, among them Arthritis Care*, the British Red Cross*, the Royal National Institute for the Blind*, and the Royal National Institute for Deaf People*.

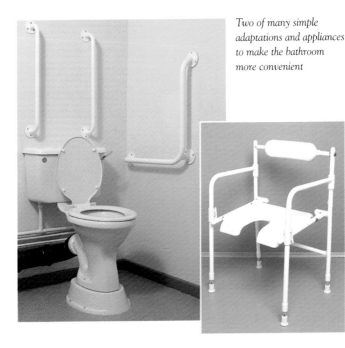

Two of many simple adaptations and appliances to make the bathroom more convenient

GETTING GRANTS

You can get a disabled facilities grant from your local authority, which will be mandatory if you can fulfil certain conditions. The work proposed must be 'necessary and appropriate to meet the needs of the disabled occupant', and must also be 'reasonable and practicable, given the age and condition of the property'. When the work has been carried out, it should give the person one or more of the following benefits, as appropriate:

◆ access into and out of the house is made easier

◆ kitchen and bathroom facilities are provided that are suitable for the independent and safe use of the person concerned

◆ the heating system has been improved, and lighting and heating controls are easier to use

◆ it is easier for the disabled person to care for another person who is dependent on them.

You can also apply for discretionary grants for a variety of improvements to make a property more amenable for an occupant with a disability. Both the mandatory and discretionary grants are subject to means-testing. Ask your local authority for details of these, as well as about renovation grants (you do not need to be elderly or disabled to qualify) and minor works assistance, which includes an Elderly Resident Adaptation grant for adapting your home so that an elderly person (someone over 60) can live with you.

Basements and cellars

Many older houses have either a basement or a cellar. Basements were built as the lowest storey of the house, and were generally intended for use as kitchens and sculleries, or for similar purposes, by live-in staff. They lie wholly or partly below ground level, while their walls continue upwards to form the ground and upper storeys. They usually have some natural light and ventilation, and access may be via a staircase within the house, or by a separate, external staircase running down a well excavated next to the building, allowing entry to the 'below stairs' area for deliveries or tradesmen. Many basements with separate entrances (found mainly in town houses) have ended up as single-storey flats. Those with access from within the house may well have fallen out of use as their structural damp-proofing failed with the passage of time and rendered them unfit for habitation.

Cellars, on the other hand, were generally built under only part of the house, and their access was always just from inside the house: either via a narrow staircase beneath the main flight of stairs, or occasionally by way of a trap door whose steps or wall ladder led down into the cellar itself. In Victorian houses, the cellar frequently extended beyond the front wall, allowing coal deliveries to be made directly into it through a coal hole set into the pavement outside. A typical cellar has no natural light or ventilation, and may possess only the most rudimentary damp-proofing.

A basement clearly offers considerable scope for conversion into habitable rooms, while the uses to which a cellar can be put are rather more restricted, unless ways can be found by which to introduce natural light, such as the excavation of wells against the house walls.

Any conversion work that you carry out will generally need Building Regulations approval, but planning permission will be needed only if a change of use is involved: for example, in the creation of a home office, a garage or a granny flat.

RULES AND REGULATIONS

A basement or cellar conversion will not need planning permission unless a change of use is involved: to a home office, a self-contained flat or a garage, for example. Any structural work will need Building Regulations approval, although you can use the building notice scheme instead of applying for written approval if you are confident that the work you are carrying out complies with the Regulations. You will also need approval if you are installing new sanitary (see Services, opposite) or fuel-burning appliances, and any new wiring work carried out should comply with the IEE Wiring Regulations.

OPTIONS

Basements

Since the basement will originally have been buil[t] for use as living space, the major problem you wi[ll] face in restoring it is likely to be that of damp. It [is] worth having a professional survey done in order t[o] expose the extent of the problem, and, if the damp [is] widespread, or if you live in an area with a hig[h] water table, you may also decide to leave any neces[s]ary remedial work to the experts (see pages 94–5[.] However, if in the end you decide to tackle the wor[k] yourself, it will involve:

1 applying liquid damp-proofer if an existing con[c]crete floor is sound
2 putting down a polythene damp-proof membran[e] (dpm), covered with a new concrete screed, o[n] top of the existing floor; or
3 lifting an existing direct-to-earth floor and layin[g] a new concrete floor, complete with integral dp[m]
4 treating the walls with liquid damp-proofer and [a] skim coat of new plaster if the existing plaster [is] sound; or
5 stripping the existing plaster and replastering th[e] walls with a damp-resistant, three-coat, plaste[r] system, similar to that used when treating above[-]ground rising damp; or
6 fixing special corrugated sheets to the walls t[o] allow the ventilation of their surfaces, and plas[-]tering over the sheets.

Apart from dealing with damp, you may have t[o] attend to other elements of the basement. These wi[ll] probably include:

♦ replacing old timber windows, door frames an[d]

Adding even a small extension is likely to wreck the part of your garden nearest the house: allow for this in your budget

FORWARD PLANNING

Finally, if you have ambitious plans for a large home extension but lack the necessary financial resources at present for carrying out your plans in their entirety, you may be able to break down the work into more manageable stages. You could, for example, decide to build only a flat-roofed, single-storey extension to begin with, but with foundations and walls that are strong enough to carry a second floor. This could be added later when funds allow, perhaps with a flat roof, which could finally be replaced with a new pitched roof to complete the project in the fullness of time.

Fireplaces

If today's new homes can be regarded as a barometer of taste, fireplaces are very much back in fashion, at least in the main living-room. In older homes there is a growing trend towards the sympathetic restoration of the house's original features, with home-owners recommissioning fireplaces that were made redundant in the central-heating boom of the 1970s, or replacing ugly or unsuitable fireplace surrounds with more traditional specimens, bought new or from architectural salvage dealers.

It is often easy to bring a disused fireplace and flue back into use

*I*f you want a fireplace in your home, there are a lot of variables to consider, and the course you could take depends on what you already have, what you want and how much construction and alteration work you are prepared to undertake. It is much easier to bring a disused fireplace and flue back into use than it is to create a new one.

Recommissioning an old fireplace does not need any sort of official permission, but there are several vital safety checks that you will need to carry out first. Creating a new fireplace and flue will need

Building Regulations approval, and you might also need planning permission to build a new chimney stack. Ask your local authority for advice at an early stage in the project.

OPTIONS

Using an existing fireplace and flue

If you have an existing fireplace and flue in your home that have simply been out of use for a number of years, you should, in theory, have little trouble in bringing them back into use. It is essential to have the flue swept and inspected by an expert – a member of the National Association of Chimney Sweeps*, for example – who will survey it and will either issue a so-called 'chimney certificate', if it is fit for use, or will recommend any necessary remedial treatment (see Chimney problems on page 112) if it is not.

You may need to improve the ventilation to the room containing the fireplace, especially if the flue does not draw well. You may also need to fit a special cowl to the chimneypot in order to help to increase the natural updraught.

You should also carefully inspect the fireback for any telltale signs of cracking. Unless it is in good condition, it would be a false economy measure not to replace it with a new fireback – a job that is well within the scope of the average do-it-yourself enthusiast in most situations.

Recommissioning a blocked-up fireplace

If the original fireplace has been removed and the opening blocked up, you may still be able to recommission it relatively easily. How much work is involved in doing so will depend on how extensively it was decommissioned in the first place.

♦ Check that the flue is still intact all the way up to the chimneypot. At the very least the flue may have been capped, and at worst the stack itself and some of the flue's brickwork within the house may have been removed. If the latter is the case, some exten-

This splendid fire surround and mantelpiece is the focal point of the room

Restoring a disused fire place can be a messy job

sive rebuilding work will be involved, although using modern block chimneys will speed up the restoration work. If the flue is intact, have it inspected and swept, as above.

♦ Open up the old fireplace by removing panelling or masonry from the original opening to see how much of it (if anything) remains. If the fireback is still in place and in sound condition, all that you will have to do is to have the flue swept and checked, and then fit a replacement fire surround and decorative hearth. If everything has been removed, you will need to fit a new fireback within the opening as well.

RULES AND REGULATIONS

You will need Building Regulations approval to install a new heating appliance that burns solid fuel or gas, and also to construct a new flue or chimney. The latter option may also need planning permission if it alters the external appearance of your home; check before you build one, especially if you live in a listed building or in a conservation area.

If you are recommissioning an existing fireplace and flue, or are installing a gas flame-effect fire, you must also satisfy the Regulations requirements concerning an adequate supply of ventilation and the safe discharge of combustion gases. Ask your local authority building inspector for advice on this.

Building a new flue

If you want a flueless fireplace, perhaps as a result of some previous extensive remodelling of your home's interior, you may be able to construct a new flue. This can be built inside or outside the house, although the latter is generally simpler and involves far less disruption than creating an internal flue. You can then create a new fireplace in the flue's location. Building a new flue is a job for a professional builder who is a chimney expert, and requires Building Regulations approval.

Creating a 'fake' fire

If you want to achieve the appearance of a real fire without any of the hassles involved in burning solid fuel, you could consider fitting a decorative, flame-effect fire. These use gas to heat a bed of special ceramic 'coals' within a traditional-looking grate, and can look extremely realistic. The fully enclosed type with a surrounding convector box is more efficient than the open-grate types. All can be fitted within a conventional fireplace opening; some can also be installed as balanced-flue appliances, allowing them to be fitted against an outside wall without the need for a chimney, and fan-assisted types can be installed up to 4m (about 13ft) away from an external wall.

CHIMNEY PROBLEMS

The two main problems affecting old chimneys are the deterioration of the stack itself, and cracks within the flue. Your inspector will be able to advise you on their condition.

An old stack is likely to need some repointing to its brickwork, and the existing pot may need to be reset with new mortar capping (called flaunching), or may need replacing altogether. Get a builder to do the job unless you are happy to work at high levels and you can set up a suitable access platform around the stack.

An old flue may not draw well because of an accumulation of débris, and may have cracks which allow smoke to seep out into other rooms in the house. It may also have suffered from condensation while out of use, leading to staining on the chimney breast along its path to the roof. The solution is to have the flue relined with an approved lining material – a job that can involve opening the flue at various points and one to leave to specialist contractors. Check with your local authority building inspector to find out which method is best for your flue.

Always have an old chimney swept before bringing it back into use

Garages

If you have a car, you really need a garage. This does not just provide a dry and secure home for your car, but can also act as a useful store for items such as ladders, lawn mowers and bicycles, can make a workshop for your DIY and car repair jobs, and can even serve as an overspill utility room for appliances such as chest freezers. Having one will certainly add to the value of your property if and when you come to sell it.

A garage is seen by many as essential. If you are planning to build one, make sure that you match it to your house style

Without the space on your plot of land to build a garage your only option is to convert part of the ground floor of the house into a built-in garage, which will entail structural upheaval and loss of living space. This option is not worth considering unless you intend to remain in the house for the foreseeable future, regard a garage as essential and can afford the loss of living space.

You may need planning permission to build a garage, depending on its situation in relation to the house. You do not generally need Building Regulations approval, unless the garage is attached to the house's wall, and is therefore in effect a home extension. Check before starting work.

OPTIONS

Building beside the house

If you have available space beside your house, the ideal solution is to build a detached garage on it, perhaps sited with one wall against the boundary of your property in order to leave a pathway between the garage and the house. For a spacious single garage you will need a strip of land about 4m (13ft) wide (including room for the path), while for a double garage you will need a strip about 6m (20ft) wide.

An alternative is to build a lean-to structure next to the house's wall, and to leave space for a path between the garage and the boundary, instead of between the garage and the house. The minimum internal width for such a garage is about 2.4m (8ft) anything less will make parking, and entering and leaving the car, very awkward. Space considerations apart, this may be a more economical solution than building a detached garage. Practically speaking, it may also be ideal if the side wall of your house has few windows that would be covered by the garage. If there is a side door, this could provide direct access to the garage from the house (but note that the door must be a fire door in this situation).

If space is very limited, you may end up completely blocking any access to the back garden from the side of the house. If this is unavoidable, include a side or rear access door within the garage so that you can get to the back garden without having to pass through the house. You should check whether local building rules allow this; some do not.

Building behind the house

If you have less than about 2.4m (8ft) of space at the side of the house, you could consider using this as an access way, instead extending your drive down the side of the house and building a detached garage in the back garden. Whether you can (or want to) do this depends on the amount of available space in your back garden, and whether you mind such

ructure dominating your outlook. You could, of
urse, disguise its presence with plants, but these
ill take time to establish themselves.

A garage in the back garden should be built with a
ap of at least 1m (3ft 3in) between it and the house.
it can be sited 5m (16ft) or more from the house,
r planning permission purposes it will be classed as
n outbuilding rather than as a home extension.

If your property has a rear access road, a garage sit-
ited at the bottom of the garden that opens on to
e access road is an ideal solution. You may even be
le to site the garage parallel to the road itself if
ur property is wide enough, so allowing you to
ive the car straight into and out of the garage.

uilding in front of the house

space beside the house, or an access route past it,
es not exist, your last resort is to site a garage in
e front garden. However, this will certainly spoil
e appearance of the house, may also possibly block
ur view of the world, and is unlikely to be accept-
le to the local planning authority unless other
roperties in the road have already established a
recedent of encroaching in front of the existing
uilding line.

HOICES OF GARAGE

nce you have made a decision about where to site
ur garage, and have cleared any planning permis-
on hurdles, you will next have to consider whether
build it from scratch or buy a kit garage.

The main advantage of building your own garage
or of getting a local builder to do the job for you –
that you can precisely satisfy your space require-
ents, easily cope with any local site difficulties, and
eate a building that is a good match for your
ouse's style. The two major disadvantages are the
me that it takes to build and, if you are employing a
uilder, the cost.

Kit garages have more advantages than disadvan-
ges. They are available in a wide range of standard
zes, with plenty of flexibility of design, and their
oks have now considerably improved on their
der, sectional predecessors. They are generally con-
derably cheaper than traditionally built garages,
nd can be erected in a day or a weekend once a suit-
le base has been laid. In short, unless you have a
articular dislike of sectional buildings, a kit garage
ill probably be your preferred choice.

The best way of choosing a kit garage is to send
r manufacturers' brochures, which are regularly

If you have space, build a detached garage in your garden

advertised in newspapers and home interest maga-
zines. It is also worth visiting any local show sites, or
asking the manufacturers to put you in touch with
past customers in your area, so that you can see the
finished buildings before making your choice.

Once you have selected the garage you want, you
could either opt to build it yourself, or you could
leave this to the manufacturer. If you choose the former route, you will be supplied with a detailed specification for the garage's base, plus full step-by-step
instructions for assembling the building. This is quite
straightforward but definitely a two-person job.

RULES AND REGULATIONS

For the purposes of planning permission, a garage is classed as a home extension if it is
attached to the house, or stands within 5m (16ft) of it. According to the permitted development rules for home extensions, this means that no permission is needed as long as the
addition of the garage does not result in breaching the permitted development allowance
(see Extensions on pages 104–9 for details). If you (or any previous owners) have already
extended your house in the past, part of the allowance may have been used up, and you
will have to apply for permission for your garage.

If the garage is built more than 5m (16 ft) from the house, it is classed as an outbuilding for planning permission purposes (see pages 144–5 for details), and far fewer
restrictions apply.

You will always have to apply for planning permission if the proposed garage is to be
sited in front of the existing building line, or if building it will result in more than half the
original garden area being covered by buildings. You will also need permission if you have
to create a new access route to the garage from a classified road (see Driveways on pages
98–101 for more details).

As far as Building Regulations approval is concerned, detached garages with a floor area
of less than 30sq m (325sq ft) are exempt from control as long as they are built wholly of
non-combustible material (as most garages are), or are otherwise at least 1m (3ft 3in) from
the property's boundary. Attached garages are classed as home extensions and must have
Building Regulations approval, especially with regard to fireproofing.

Granny flats

If you have a family member who is elderly or who has some sort of disability, you may need to provide accommodation for him or her within your home. One way of doing this is to create a so-called 'granny' flat: self-contained living quarters that offer a degree of privacy to someone who is capable of living independently on an everyday basis, but who may need support close at hand from time to time. Such a flat may also be an attractive way of providing accommodation for grown-up children. It is most important to involve the person who will be occupying the flat at all the planning stages.

If space is restricted, the essential kitchen units and appliances could be positioned in an alcove or along the wall of the living-room

The type of accommodation that you could create will obviously depend on the type, size and layout of your house; some buildings will lend themselves more readily to conversion than others. It is worth getting professional advice on this point, since an architect may have ideas and suggestions that you had not even considered.

You are likely to require both planning permission and Building Regulations approval to create a granny flat within your home. Ask your local authority for advice before your plans progress beyond outline form.

OPTIONS

Using existing rooms

If your house is big enough, you should have little difficulty in finding enough space for a self-contained flat. You could choose adjacent rooms on either the ground or first floor, for example, using one as the flat's living-room and the other as its bedroom. The conversion work will involve:

1 blocking up the existing bedroom's doorway
2 creating a new door between the two rooms
3 partitioning part of the bedroom to serve as an en suite bathroom
4 partitioning part of the living-room to create a kitchenette
5 altering the wiring, plumbing and heating as necessary for serving the new layout.

The layout of your house may also lend itself to other ways of using existing rooms.

Converting the loft

If your roof's structure is suitable, a loft conversion is an ideal way in which to create extra living space within the house; it may not be the best solution as a flat for an elderly relative who finds climbing stairs hard work, however. A better way of using the new space is probably to move your own living quarters up one floor, and to allocate rooms on the ground floor to the flat. (See *Loft conversions* on pages 138–43 for details of what is involved.)

Converting a basement

The type of semi-basement that was built in some older town houses for use as servants' quarters is ideal for conversion into a self-contained flat, since it usually has its own entrance, as well as windows in the main rooms. Other basement areas, built primarily as storage cellars, may be suitable if they are damp-

proofed and natural light can be admitted, but will require considerably more work in order to make them habitable. (See *Basements and cellars* on pages 66–7 for more details.)

Converting a garage

If your house has an integral garage (within the house's walls) or an attached one, converting it into living accommodation is relatively straightforward. The space is, by definition, already self-contained, and its position makes it easy to create access and extend the household's services to it. The conversion work will involve:

1 removing the garage door and replacing it with a window which has either a masonry or timber-frame infill beneath it
2 installing additional windows as necessary
3 altering the access route from the house, or from outside, into the conversion
4 putting down a damp-proof membrane (dpm) and thermal insulation, and then laying a new screed on the floor, or installing a timber floor on top of it
5 insulating and lining the walls and ceiling of an attached garage
6 plastering the walls and ceiling of an integral garage
7 building internal partition walls as required
8 extending the house's wiring, plumbing and heating services as necessary
9 fitting and finishing the conversion to suit the occupant's requirements.

Building an extension

If none of these options is feasible in your circumstances, your last resort is to build an extension. As long as you have the space (and the money), this is possibly the best solution, because the extension can be tailor-made to suit its occupant's requirements. It can have its own access route, or can be linked with the existing house if you prefer. (See *Extensions* on pages 104–9 for more details.)

SERVICES

Wiring

The amount of wiring work that you will have to carry out will of course depend on the nature of the conversion. If you are using existing rooms, you will

RULES AND REGULATIONS

Creating a granny flat will probably require planning permission, since it will result in a change of use (see pages 84–7). However, if the conversion is purely an interior one, and has no separate external means of access, permission may not be needed. Ask your local authority for advice before proceeding with your plans.

The conversion will also have to meet the requirements of the Building Regulations, although if you are confident of complying with them you can use the quick building notice method instead of applying for formal approval. There is one exception: you must apply for formal approval if you are converting the loft in a building of two or more storeys.

Remember that if you have a mortgage you must seek the mortgage lender's permission before carrying out the conversion. You may, in any case, need to increase your mortgage in order to pay for the work. Do not forget to tell your house insurance company about the changes when the work is completed.

An en suite bathroom is an ideal arrangement in a self-contained flat

Visit kitchen showrooms to get ideas for maximising the storage potential and ease of use of a small kitchen

have to do little more than add or reposition some light switches, fittings and socket outlets. In other conversions, you may be able simply to extend the house's lighting and power circuits. However, it is worth considering giving the flat its own consumer unit, supplied from a service connection box next to the main house's unit. This is essential if you are going to be installing electric water or space heating in the new flat.

Plumbing and heating

You will have to extend the existing hot and cold water supplies into the flat, including a mains pressure supply of drinking water to the kitchenette, but this work should pose few problems. Fit a gas or electric water heater if extending the existing supplies would be too disruptive.

Getting rid of waste water could present greater difficulties. If reaching the existing soil stacks and gullies will mean using overlong pipe runs, you would do well to consider using a pumped waste macerator, which will discharge water over quite long distances through small-bore waste pipes that are easier to conceal within the house's structure than large-diameter soil pipes.

If you are creating the granny flat by taking over existing rooms, you may want to reposition the radiators within them. Add small electric wall-mounted fan-heaters to the flat's bathroom and kitchenette rather than extending the existing heating system. If you are making new living space, you must check whether you can extend your heating system in order to supply it. If you cannot do so, consider fitting night storage heaters in the flat.

Cooking facilities

Plan the kitchen area meticulously, making use of some of the many space-saving fittings available in order to provide maximum storage space. If you find that it is impossible to create a separate kitchen, turn one living-room into a kitchen-diner, with units and appliances positioned in a corner or ranged along one wall.

Depending on the occupant's cooking requirements, you could fit a small hob and a microwave oven with integral grill instead of a full-sized cooker. A small counter-top fridge could provide adequate cold-food storage space. A waste disposal unit will reduce trips to the dustbin, and an extractor fan will help to disperse cooking smells.

Bathing facilities

Even if the occupant can share the main house's bathing facilities, the flat will still need a WC and washbasin as an absolute minimum. However, if space allows, it is better to incorporate either a shower cubicle or a small bath. Fit an extractor fan in the bathroom in order to minimise condensation problems. Remember that a bathroom must not open directly into a kitchen; if this arrangement is unavoidable, you will have to create a small lobby between the two rooms.

Home offices

Working from home is becoming a way of life for an increasing number of people, whether they are teleworking for a large organisation or running their own businesses. For some, the job may require little more than a desk and a telephone, but most people will have to find a space in their homes that they can convert into a fully functioning, self-contained office, with all the necessary fittings and essential telecommunications equipment.

If you have an unused room, some simple and homely furniture can turn it into a comfortable office

In principle, you will need to apply for planning permission in order to work from home, since doing so involves a change of the house's use from purely residential accommodation. In practice, many local authorities are aware of the growing trend for traditional office work to be carried out from a home base, and are prepared to allow it as long as there are no outward signs of such a business being operated from a residential property. Only if you receive regular deliveries or visitors, store and sell goods, annoy the neighbours or alter the character of the street are you likely to need formal permission. The best course of action is to contact your local authority planning department and ask for its views on your individual situation.

OPTIONS

Converting a spare room

The ideal way of creating a home office is to use an existing spare (or under-used) room for the purpose. In most homes this will probably be a bedroom, which has the advantage that it separates the office space from the living-rooms during the working day.

If you have separate living- and dining-rooms, and the dining-room is used only on special occasions, it may make sense to convert it to office use if meals can be easily served elsewhere in the house – in the kitchen, for example. To keep the room available for occasional dining use, you could retain the dining table as a work surface and disperse the chairs elsewhere in the house.

If your house has large rooms, you may be able to partition an existing room in order to create space for an office. Building an insulated, timber-framed partition wall and door opening into the new space is relatively simple. You will, however, need to ensure that both halves of the newly partitioned room have (or could be given) a window: working in a window-less box, even if it is mechanically ventilated, is hardly good for the soul.

Converting the loft

If you have unused loft space that would be suitable for conversion into an office, this is an option worth considering. It will keep the new office separate from the rest of the house, and, unlike converting a spare room, will not reduce the amount of available living space. You will need to provide access to the loft conversion, of course, but using a 'space-saver' staircase will minimise the disruption and loss of space that this will cause.

As long as the loft is suitable for conversion, creating a room and providing daylight through one or more roof windows is a relatively straightforward task. Extending the existing electrical circuits for lighting and power supplies and some electrical space heating will be simple, and you will not need to make any alterations to the household's plumbing systems. (See pages 138–43 for more details.) The conversion will need Building Regulations approval, and may also require planning permission.

Converting a garage

If you have an integral or attached garage, and are prepared to park the car on the driveway, you could convert the garage to office use. Its position makes it easy to create access from the house if none already exists, and also to extend the existing household services as necessary. The conversion work will involve:

1 damp-proofing, insulating and screeding the garage floor
2 removing the garage door and filling the opening to include a window
3 insulating and lining the walls and ceiling of an attached garage; or
4 plastering the walls and the existing ceiling of an integral garage.

You may need Building Regulations approval for the conversion; check with your local authority before proceeding with the work. Also check to see whether planning permission is required for the change of use.

If you have a detached garage, this could also be converted for use as an office, but the structure will probably need extensive damp-proofing, draught-proofing and insulation beforehand. Whether this is feasible or cost-effective depends on the state of the existing structure. You will also have to consider the problems of extending the electricity supplies and telephone/fax line(s) to the site. It may be better to build yourself a separate office elsewhere in the garden, or to consider using the existing garage site for a completely new outbuilding that is better suited to your requirements.

Building a garden office

If you have neither the space within the house nor a loft or garage that is suitable for conversion, you could consider building an office in your garden, if you have the room. This could be a purpose-built masonry structure, or a prefabricated building; a number of firms now offer attractive solid timber

Make sure you have enough work surfaces for all your office equipment

buildings that are suitable for use all year round.

You will almost certainly need planning permission to build a dedicated home office on your land, since it cannot be classed as an outbuilding connected with the residential use of the house in the same way as swimming-pool enclosures or summerhouses. The building will be exempt from Building Regulations control, however, as long as it has a floor area which does not exceed 30sq m (325sq ft), is at least 1m (3ft 3in) from the property's boundary, and is built wholly of non-combustible materials.

Building an extension

If you have the available space, an alternative to building a separate garden office is to erect a small home extension at the side or back of the house. It could have its own access door, or be linked to the house. It will be subject to the same planning permission and Building Regulations requirements as any home extension (see pages 104–9).

EQUIPPING A HOME OFFICE

The type of equipment that you will need for furnishing your home office will depend on the nature of your business. At the very least you will need a

work surface, a chair and some storage space. Yo could use existing furniture for this, but it pays to be a comfortable office chair and some proper filin cabinets, perhaps second-hand. A length of lami nate-covered kitchen worktop makes an ideal wo surface, and could span two low-level filing cabine to form a spacious desk. As far as other types of sto age units are concerned, a wide choice of modul and flat-pack furniture is available.

Make sure that your office is well lit and has enoug power points, and extend the existing facilities necessary. Do not be tempted to use a multitude adaptors from which to run electrical equipment you risk overloading the outlet and causing a fire.

Finally, you are certain to need a telephone lin Have a separate line installed, so that you can kee business and family calls separate, and buy a answerphone for your business line so that you ca receive messages when you are out.

If you need a fax machine, a switchable mod that shares your telephone line will be adequate fe many people. If you use a computer that needs to b linked to others via a modem, it will pay to install second, dedicated line, so that any communicatic with it will not be continually interrupted by phor or fax messages.

A home office with a view of the garden is a far more relaxing place to work than any city office

Kitchens

The kitchen is probably the most regularly improved room in the house, and the one on which most money is spent – or wasted. Completely refitting a typical kitchen can cost thousands of pounds, yet most home-owners list improving their kitchen as one of their top priorities. The key to getting the sort of kitchen you want is to analyse your needs very carefully. Aim for a kitchen that suits the way in which you and your family use the room. This will help you to focus on what is wrong with your kitchen at present, and may help to save you a great deal of unnecessary expense too. Here are some of the options you could choose.

A fitted kitchen can be given its own individual style with some careful design

OPTIONS

Refitting the kitchen from scratch

An entire refit is the option that the kitchen planners and suppliers want you to take: pulling out the existing fixtures and starting again with an empty room. If your kitchen is a disaster area with a badly planned layout, old-fashioned units and wiring and plumbing facilities from a bygone age, this is probably the best option. However, it will be expensive if you do the work yourself, and very expensive if you employ someone to install everything for you.

Updating the kitchen

If your kitchen has been fitted out relatively recently, but is beginning to look rather shabby and dated, there may be little wrong with its skeleton – the units themselves – and nothing wrong with the layout. If the units are basically plastic-coated, chipboard boxes, as long as they were properly installed, they seldom wear out. There seems little point in throwing away one set of perfectly sound boxes just to replace them with another, near-identical set, when you can give the room a new look by fitting new door and drawer fronts to the existing units.

You may want to take such a refurbishment a step further and replace the worktops too, perhaps incorporating a new sink unit while you are doing so. Once the room has been redecorated and has been given some new accessories – new blinds and light fittings, for example, or even a new floor covering – the kitchen will look as though it has been completely refitted, but the project will have cost a fraction of the price of a full-scale refit, and will have taken far less time.

Enlarging the kitchen

If your existing kitchen is very small, even the most ingenious planning will not make it appear significantly larger. You will therefore have to consider creating more space by extending the room, either outwards into a single-storey extension, if you have the room, or else by taking over some adjacent floor space from within the house itself.

You may have an adjoining utility room, pantry or scullery, for example, which you could incorporate into the existing kitchen by breaching or knocking down the dividing wall. Another possible alternative is to turn the existing kitchen and an adjoining dining-room into a large kitchen-diner – the 'breakfasting kitchen' so beloved by estate agents as a term for a kitchen that is big enough to eat in.

Peninsular units separate a cooking area neatly

Relocating the kitchen

The final option if you do not want to contemplate knocking down internal walls is to relocate the kitchen to another room in the house: for example, it might make good sense to bring the kitchen to the front of the house and have your living-room at the back. Alternatively, you could swap round the facilities in your existing kitchen and dining-room, so making better use of the generally larger, but often under-used, dining-room to create the kitchen you really want.

The main consideration with this type of conversion is the provision of wiring, plumbing and waste disposal services to the relocated kitchen. The first two services generally pose few problems, but if your drains are at the rear of the house, arranging waste disposal could involve creating a new drain run from the front of the house. If you are contemplating this option, examine all the potential pitfalls first, and get professional help if necessary to find the best solution to the problem.

Glazed and open units are an alternative to solid doors

KITCHEN PLANNING

The size and age of your family are two of the most important factors in determining the sort of kitchen that you will need; a family with three small children has very different requirements to the bachelor gourmet, for example. So the first step is to record a typical day in the life of your kitchen. Here are some questions to ask yourself as you do so.

Breakfast Is this a family meal, or is your kitchen treated like a fast-food takeaway? Do you want room to allow formal seating round a table, or something less space-consuming, like a breakfast bar? Indeed, do you want to eat in the kitchen at all?

Laundry Have you always had your washing-machine in the kitchen? Do you really want it there, or would it make more sense (and help to streamline your daily activities) to move your laundry facilities somewhere else? The planner's first choice is usually to add a utility room, but this is not necessarily very logical – after all, how often do you undress downstairs? Especially if you have small children, it may be more sensible for the laundry facilities to be closer to the bathroom or bedrooms instead.

Shopping When you stagger back from the supermarket, do you always curse the lack of available space on which to dump and unpack your shopping?

Life would be much easier if you could provide additional worktop space close to your main food storage area. The provision of a new side or back door, with easy access to the car-parking space, would mean that you would not have to carry heavy shopping through the house from the front door all the way to the kitchen.

Child-minding If you have toddlers at home all day, you will want to keep an eye on them while they play, without having them under your feet. A combined kitchen-diner would provide convenient indoor playing space.

Other meals Where are lunch and your evening meal eaten? Do you intend keeping the dining-room for special occasions only, with the family usually eating together in the kitchen? If you use your dining-room regularly, is the route from the kitchen a sensible one when carrying trays or hot dishes, or wheeling a trolley? Do you want to combine the two rooms, with perhaps a large hatch or peninsula unit placed between them?

Entertainment Do you spend a lot of the day in the kitchen? If so, plan to include a television, radio or mini hi-fi equipment somewhere in the room. It is also a good idea to install a telephone extension in the kitchen, perhaps complete with a speakerphone facility, so that you can still manage calls when you have your hands full.

Once you have answers to questions like these, you have got the first stage of your kitchen planning off to the right start. Now you can start working things out in more detail.

What shape should the kitchen be?

There are several traditional options for kitchen layouts, including the following.

♦ The single-line layout groups everything in the room along one straight wall – this is not generally a practical solution, except in very small rooms with minimal facilities.

♦ The galley kitchen usually has sink, cooker and some worktops along one wall, and food storage and preparation areas along the opposite wall. This layout can work well, but if the room is a through route to the back door, you will need plenty of floor space down the middle of it.

♦ The L-shaped room has fixtures and fittings along two adjacent walls. This can be very effective, providing space in the opposite corner of the room for a table and chairs if the room is big enough, as well as separating the work areas from any through traffic to the back door.

This in-line kitchen keeps the traffic route to the back door clear of obstructions

This U-shaped kitchen features some base units that are accessible from both sides

♦ The U-shaped room has its equipment and work-tops ranged along three walls. It is a highly efficient plan, and can be used to link kitchen and dining areas if one section of the 'U' acts as a peninsula unit. However, this layout can entail a lot of walking about if the room is large, and, in a small room, can be very cramped for more people than just one cook and bottle-washer.

♦ The island layout sites units or a table in the centre of an L- or U-shaped floor plan. This can be very effective in a kitchen which is used a great deal for family activities, but needs careful planning and plenty of space in order to avoid a troublesome congestion of people round the island.

If your previous kitchen layout worked well, it is better to stick to the formula that you know and like and to design your new kitchen round a familiar lay-out. If it was a disaster, however, now is the time to try a more practical layout.

Which appliances should be installed?

Once the kitchen is beginning to take shape, you will need to start thinking about the equipment that you want to include, and where best to site each item within the room's layout.

Start with the sink. This should ideally be sited against an outside wall so that waste pipes can be plumbed in easily, and it is also desirable for it to be placed beneath a window. Try to keep it away from corners, so that there is plenty of room to get to it, and also so that there is space for one person to stand and dry dishes while another washes up. If the sink is on the same side of the room as the cooker, try to include an uninterrupted run of work surfaces between hob and sink.

The sink configuration that you select is largely a matter of taste. Whether you have a dishwasher or not, make sure that the sink's bowl is big enough to hold large roasting dishes and oven trays; many

The traditional dresser and table can look stunning even in a modern kitchen

You can hide appliances behind decor door panels

provision for the extraction of steam and cooking smells from the kitchen. A ducted cooker hood, or an extractor fan, are ideal solutions.

Other appliances divide into two groups: those requiring plumbing and waste connections, and those needing only a power supply. Included in the first group are washing machines, combined washer/driers and dishwashers; all are best sited against an external wall, or close to one if against an internal wall, in order to keep waste-pipe runs short. Try to site a dishwasher close to the sink for the convenient loading of dirty dishes; its outlet can generally be linked into the sink's waste pipe.

The second group includes tumble driers, fridges and freezers. If you have a tumble drier, it must have a vent to the outside air (as must a washer/drier), unless your model is a condensing type. Remember that most tumble driers can be stacked on top of a washing machine, thus economising on wall space.

The only other appliance with special space requirements is the fridge, since with many models you need to be able to open the door beyond a right angle in order to remove the shelves and drawers, and the door does not usually open fully within the width of the appliance. This means that it cannot be sited in corners.

All floor-standing kitchen appliances (with the exception of large chest freezers) occupy a floor space of 600sq mm (just under 2sq ft), which means that planning them is often merely a question of providing enough 'parking' spaces for your present (and future) needs. Chest freezers, with their lift-up lids, do not really belong in kitchens anyway: they are much better sited in a utility room, larder or garage if you have one.

Finally, there is one further appliance which you may already have in your kitchen, or which you may want to replace as part of your kitchen refurbishment: the central heating boiler. Compact, modern wall-mounted gas-fired units with balanced flues can be built unobtrusively into a run of wall units, and do not even have to be situated against an outside wall any more, thanks to the introduction of fanned-flue boilers.

Which units should be fitted?

You are now in a position to start thinking in millimetres – in other words, to start making everything fit into place. You have decided upon the style, layout and contents of your new kitchen, so what remains now is the detailed planning. Next choose your units.

bowl-and-a-half sinks have rather small main bowls, and the half-bowl is often hardly big enough to rinse cutlery, although it can be useful for food preparation if its outlet is fitted with a waste-disposal unit. However, a waste-disposal unit can be equally well positioned beneath the main bowl.

Think about the cooker next. Much will depend on your preference for freestanding or built-in equipment. The former is generally cheaper to buy, and can be taken with you when you move house. The latter offers greater planning flexibility, since you can site the hob and oven separately, and you can also avoid low-level ovens and grills if you prefer, by building them into tall storage units instead of siting them below worktop level.

If possible, keep freestanding cookers or built-in hobs away from corners or the end of a run of units: you need worktop space at either side of the hob for safety reasons. More importantly, never site a cooker or hob in front of a window, because leaning across a hot hob could be dangerous, and air currents could blow out gas burners.

Once you have decided what types of appliance to install, and where to site them, remember to make

This huge kitchen has ample room for a table and chairs in the centre

Most kitchen manufacturers have at last standardised the dimensions of their units, using a 600sq mm (just under 2sq ft) module for base units, and one of 600x300mm for wall units. Base units are a standard height of 900mm, but you can raise or lower them to suit your own height by adapting the plinth design. Wall units may be described as 'standard' (600mm high) or 'tall' (800 or 900mm high, reaching almost to the ceiling). Double units are 1200mm wide, although some firms also offer narrower 500

and 1000mm units, as well as a range of 'infill' units in narrower sizes.

The choice of materials used in the units is very much a personal decision, but it is important to keep practical considerations to the fore. Worktops need to be hard-wearing yet easy to clean, while door and drawer fronts may have to stand up to everything from collisions with children's wheeled toys to attacks from the family dog. Natural wood finishes may be the interior designers' favourite finish, but

A breakfast bar acts as an attractive divider in this small kitchen

here are plenty of attractive laminate finishes that are likely to be cheaper and longer-lasting.

As you begin to draw up a floor plan, remember that the ranges of many kitchen manufacturers now include integrated appliances – items such as fridges, freezers and dishwashers, which can be fitted with fascia panels so that they blend with the rest of the kitchen's base units. Choosing integrated appliances may, however, limit your freedom of choice as far as the individual appliances are concerned.

Once you have decided on the range of units that you plan to install, it is time to create a detailed scale plan that allocates everything to its place, and ensures that it all fits. You can do this yourself, but even if you plan to install the kitchen yourself, you can generally make use of the supplier's planning service – nowadays often a computerised system that lets you visualise in three dimensions how your kitchen will look.

What about services?

When you are refitting a kitchen from scratch, you have the chance to reorganise and tidy up the existing plumbing, waste disposal and electrical services, and also to extend them if necessary.

Most of the plumbing will run through the space between the back of base units and the wall, so take this opportunity to insulate any pipes that run against cold, outside walls. Fit mini gate valves on the pipe runs to the sink's taps and to all water-using appliances, so that you can easily isolate them for maintenance and repairs. Finally, make sure that all exposed metalwork is safely crossbonded to earth. Be sure to call in a professional electrician to advise you about this aspect if you are at all unsure about how to go about it.

As far as the electricity supplies to the kitchen are concerned, the ideal solution is to have a 30-amp ring-main circuit supplying that room alone, on account of the large number of high-powered appliances within it. Make sure that you have ample socket outlets situated above worktop level with which to serve small portable appliances, and fit unswitched outlets in appliance recesses as spurs controlled by double-pole switches above the worktop. While you are doing any necessary wiring work, provide a power supply for an electric cooker, even if you use gas.

Finally, you will want to provide lighting at ceiling level for the whole room, and also task lighting above worktops, hobs and sinks. It is easiest to install the former by extending the main house's lighting

A stylish tailor-made sideboard separates the kitchen and dining area

circuits, and to supply the latter as a spur from the kitchen's ring-main circuit.

Finishing touches

The final step to take in the planning of your new kitchen is to finalise the details of the decor. Floor coverings need to be durable yet easy to keep clean, and should ideally also be warm underfoot.

Similar criteria apply to the wall and ceiling surfaces. Stick to materials that will wear well and will be easy to clean. Avoid materials with textured finishes, and think twice about using wall coverings rather than paint: there is rarely an unobstructed section of wall in the average kitchen. Ceramic tiles are a practical, if more expensive, alternative to paint for areas such as splashbacks and the wall surfaces above worktops.

RULES AND REGULATIONS

Unless you are carrying out major structural alterations when creating your new kitchen, the only rules with which you need to comply are the Building Regulations requirements concerning making new waste disposal arrangements and fitting new heating appliances. If the work will involve either of these, contact your local building control officer for advice before proceeding.

Any new wiring work should comply with the requirements of the IEE Wiring Regulations in England and Wales, and must do so in Scotland. Unless you are a competent DIY electrician, call in a professional to carry out and test any new wiring work.

Lighting

Good lighting goes hand in hand with the whole field of interior design, since the type and colour of your home's lighting can have a dramatic effect on how walls, ceilings, floors and furnishings look. Yet the lighting systems of most homes have changed little in decades. A single central pendant light with a decorative shade is still often the only permanent fitting in a room, perhaps augmented by table or standard lamps. The more daring schemes may have a pair of wall lights here and there, but little else.

A variety of different lighting effects make this large hall a splendid room in its own right

The best way of finding out what is possible in the way of lighting is to do some research. You could start with a book on home lighting design, which will explain how lighting works, and will suggest ways in which to achieve particular lighting effects. It will also familiarise you with the huge range of light fittings available – fittings that become part of the room's furnishings rather than being just a light source.

The next step is to keep your eyes open in public places for imaginative and unusual lighting ideas, many of which can be easily transplanted into the home. As you look around, make notes of the types of lighting that you like (and dislike), and how they are achieved.

Lighting performs three main functions. A well-planned lighting scheme fulfils all three, and requires different types of light fittings for different jobs. They are to:
♦ provide background lighting, in effect taking the place of daylight when the sun sets
♦ illuminate specific tasks: this is seen in the lighting above a kitchen worktop, for example, or in reading lights on a desk or above a bed
♦ achieve a decorative effect, making individual rooms look inviting, and highlighting their interior design features.

OPTIONS

Background lighting

Background lighting needs to be discreet. The best way of achieving this is to let light bounce off surfaces, using fittings such as wall-mounted uplighters or perimeter lighting with which to 'wash' walls and ceilings with light. The important thing is to avoid glare (which not only dazzles the eyes but casts ugly shadows), by concealing the fittings from direct view, and by diffusing the light that they emit.

Task lighting

Task lighting needs to be more direct, illuminating a localised area of the room sufficiently brightly for you to be able to carry out whatever you are doing without causing eyestrain. Brightness is not the whole story, however: again, glare and harsh shadows should be avoided by means of a careful choice of style of fitting, and this will depend very much on the nature of individual tasks. For example, ceiling-mounted downlighters can illuminate a kitchen sink or hob without causing glare or shadows, while a wall-mounted or freestanding adjustable lamp

Good lighting should avoid glare and harsh shadows

behind a chair or bed is ideal for throwing light on close-work tasks such as reading or sewing.

Decorative lighting

Decorative lighting gives you a freer hand, since you are choosing optional extras rather than essentials. Here the object is to use a combination of tone and direction with which to create the desired lighting effect: for example, using spotlights with which to highlight an alcove or a picture. The light fitting itself also becomes part of the room's furnishings, whether it is lit or not.

CHOOSING FITTINGS

As you begin to build up a picture of the lighting requirements of the rooms in your home, turn your attention to selecting the fittings that you will need.
♦ Pendant fittings range from plain, pendant lampholders to multi-light fittings suspended from the ceiling by chains or rods. Some give a general, diffused light, while others direct the light mainly upwards or downwards, depending on the style of shade fitted. Rise-and-fall fittings are pendant lights with a spring-loaded, extending flex, and are popular for use over dining tables.
♦ Close-ceiling fittings are mounted on the ceiling's surface, and so emit light only in a downward direction. They usually have a translucent glass or plastic cover (the diffuser). This group includes most fluorescent light fittings, and also the various types of tracked lighting systems into which special fittings

Safely recessed bathroom lighting casts soft pools of light

can be plugged where required in order to provide local or general lighting.

♦ Wall-mounted fittings range from simple brackets holding one or more light bulbs, with or without decorative shades, to spotlights and uplighters. Plain wall lights and uplighters are mainly used for background lighting, while spotlights can provide task or decorative lighting, according to their position.

♦ Concealed fittings include downlighters, wall-washers and eyeball spotlights, and are usually recessed into the ceiling. Downlighters provide a fairly well-defined pool of light directed at the floor, while wall-washers have either an adjustable aperture or a swivelling mount that directs light downwards and to one side, so allowing the fitting to 'wash' a nearby wall with light, or to highlight an individual feature.

♦ Freestanding fittings need little explanation. This group includes table and standard lamps, which can provide background, task or decorative lighting, according to their design and position in the room, and freestanding uplighters which bounce reflected light off the ceiling and wall surfaces.

Most light fittings are designed to run off mains voltage electricity, but increasing use is also being made of extra-low-voltage fittings powered by a small transformer, especially when providing decorative lighting effects. These run at 12 volts, which means that their circuitry is intrinsically much safer than that of circuits on mains voltage, and they use small, halogen bulbs that give a brilliant white light.

They are generally more expensive to buy than mains voltage lamps, but cost a lot less to run.

On this last point, the increasing use of compact fluorescent lamps in place of conventional tungsten filament lamps also offers you the chance to enjoy considerable savings in terms of their long life and reduced running costs (once their initially higher purchase price has been absorbed).

WORKING ON THE WIRING

Most homes have one or two lighting circuits, each rated at 5 amps, that are capable of supplying a maximum of about 10 lighting points. You will probably be nearing saturation point in this respect, so adding extra light fittings will entail providing one or more new lighting circuits too. Installing these will involve a certain amount of disruption, including gaining access to floor voids and cutting chases in walls for wall-mounted fittings, not to mention providing extra fuseways in the main fuse box for the new circuits. Unless you are a fairly skilled DIY electrician, leave any work on these new circuits to a professional.

You can also run new light fittings from existing power circuits, using fused spurs. These are linked to the circuit in the same way as spur sockets, but the spur cable terminates at a fused connection unit (fcu), which is fitted with a 5-amp fuse. If this has a switch, it can be used to control all the lights on the spur circuit, which is useful for any wall lights that you want to control independently of the room's other lights. You can also use this method to power transformers running low-voltage lighting.

The last option to consider is the provision of a separate socket circuit for table and standard lamps. These do not need to be plugged into 13-amp socket outlets supplied by a ring circuit; instead, you could run a separate radial circuit from a 5-amp fuseway, supplying a number of special 2-amp socket outlets which receive the matching, round-pin plugs. This arrangement will prevent anyone plugging a more powerful appliance into your dedicated lighting circuit, and will free any existing 13-amp outlets for use by other appliances.

Finally, do not forget the extra flexibility created by using dimmer switches for controlling individual lights. It is usually simple to fit a dimmer in place of a conventional on/off switch, but remember that you will need special dimmers to control fluorescent lighting, including those fittings that contain compact fluorescent lamps.

A wall-mounted striplight is ideal for illuminating a favourite picture

Loft conversions

The majority of houses and bungalows in Britain have a loft, but few are used for anything other than storage. Yet in a typical two-storey house, converting the loft could increase the building's overall usable floor area by up to 40 per cent (depending on the roof's pitch), and in a bungalow you could gain as much as 75 per cent in extra space. More importantly, you can do this far more cheaply than by building a home extension of the same floor area, even supposing that you have room on your plot, because the 'envelope' of your new living space is already there in the shape of the loft's floor and the roof's structure.

Most lofts offer enormous potential for conversions to more living space for a growing family

*A*ll that you have to do – in principle, at least – is to gain access to the roof space, put in some windows, and then add walls, floors and ceilings to create one or more new rooms. It is often not quite as simple as that, of course, and you will have to do a certain amount of careful planning and investigative work in order to discover what is possible in your house.

OPTIONS

Deciding on the end use

The first thing that you must decide is the end use to which you intend to put your loft space. For example, you may want little more than an occasional playing area for the children – somewhere where they can lay out a train set without it getting in everyone's way, for example. Alternatively, you may want to turn it into a hobbies room – for instance, a place in which to keep the knitting machine, set up your easel permanently, or develop your own photographs. This sort of 'non-habitable' use will involve relatively little in the way of large-scale structural work, and the conversion can generally be carried out quickly and cheaply.

On the other hand, you may decide that you want proper habitable rooms – an extra bedroom or two, a teenager's bedsitter, a home office or a granny flat, for example – with all the plumbing, heating and wiring amenities that the rest of the house enjoys. This is a more complex project altogether, since the alterations will have to comply with the requirements of the Building Regulations (see below) as far as aspects such as the strength of the floors, the sound and heat insulation, ventilation and means of escape in the event of fire are concerned. It will involve considerably more work than creating a playroom or workshop, but the requirements can usually be met in one way or another.

Assessing its feasibility

Whether you can actually convert your loft depends on the structure of the roof of your house. Until the 1960s, pitched roofs were constructed on site from a framework of rafters (the sloping beams that support the roof's covering), purlins (the horizontal beams that tie the rafters together) and struts (that brace the purlins against the first-floor ceiling joists and any internal load-bearing walls). Viewed from within the loft, such a roof structure may look like an awkward place in which to fit a new room, but it can generally be easily adapted by relocating the struts

Make sure loft stairwells are properly guarded

and other components within the roof's space. However, this is a job that needs professional assessment in order to ensure that the alterations do not weaken the roof's structure.

In more recently built houses, the roof is usually constructed with roof trusses. These are prefabricated, triangular, timber frames which span the walls of the main house, so removing the need for internal load-bearing walls. The way in which the trusses are erected and braced, however, means that removing

RULES AND REGULATIONS

Planning permission is not generally needed for a loft conversion, except in Scotland, unless you plan to raise the roof's level above that of the original house, or to include dormer windows in the roof's slope facing the road. If you plan to include dormers and your house has already used up most, or all, of the permitted development allowance for home extensions (see page 30), check with your planning department in case an application for permission is deemed necessary. You will always need to apply for planning permission if you live in a listed building, a national park or an area of outstanding natural beauty.

Building Regulations approval is always required for a full-scale loft conversion in order to ensure that the alterations satisfy the requirements concerning everything from structural safety to access, heat and sound insulation, fireproofing, ventilation, waste disposal (if the conversion will contain washing, bathing or WC facilities) and, above all, means of escape in the event of fire. If the conversion is in a two-storey building, you must submit full plans and wait for approval to be granted, but you can use the building notice method for conversions in bungalows. (See Part 4 for more details.)

Roof windows are easy to fit, and can be cleaned from inside the loft

will take up some existing floor space. The design and siting of the staircase can be the most difficult part of planning a loft conversion, and it is worth seeking professional advice on this point if there is no obvious solution to the difficulties posed by your particular property.

Apart from any siting problems that you may have, your new flight of stairs must comply with the requirements of the Building Regulations concerning fire safety, and the provision of a protected means of escape (see page 142 for details). Again, professional advice is essential to ensure that you satisfy these requirements.

Strengthening the structure

The floor of most lofts is built with joists that are strong enough to carry the weight of the ceilings below, but not to support the loading from above that new loft rooms will impose. For this reason it is almost always necessary to strengthen the structure; the most common way of doing so is by installing new and deeper joists between the existing ceiling joists, and then packing them up so that they span the space between the load-bearing walls without touching the existing ceiling. An independent floor of this type also improves the sound insulation between the loft and the storey below. For more on this see pages 160–1.

If the span between the load-bearing walls is too great to allow timber joists to be used, you may be able to position steel supporting beams (RSJs) outside the usable area of the loft room and above the existing ceiling, and then to suspend the new floor joists from the beams.

Letting in light

The two most common ways of creating windows in loft rooms are to install some in the plane of the roof's slope, or to build projecting dormers. Roof windows are designed in sizes that match the standard rafter spacings; narrow models fit between adjacent pairs of rafters, while wider ones require the removal of a section of rafter. Dormer windows are built out from the roof's slope, and have a conventional, vertical window fitted between the sides of the dormer under a flat, sloping or ridged dormer roof. So-called 'bay' dormers extend to the eaves and help to create additional headroom within the loft. In theory, a dormer can also span the full width of the property, but this rarely looks attractive, and you may have trouble getting your local planning authority to agree to the scheme.

any of their components will seriously weaken the roof's structure, and therefore altering it to allow the creation of loft rooms will be difficult and expensive. Unless you are prepared to go to these lengths, all that you can realistically do is to provide improved access to, and lighting of, the roof space, and then use it for storage purposes.

Providing access

Assuming that your roof appears to be suitable for conversion, the next major decision that you will have to make is how to provide access to the loft space. If the conversion will provide new, habitable rooms, you will need a proper staircase (or, at the very least, a flight of 'space-saver' stairs with cut-away treads). You may be able to position this above and parallel to your existing staircase if there is sufficient headroom in the loft above the stairwell. If there is not, you may have to construct a dormer over the stairwell in order to provide the necessary headroom. If this option is impossible, the new flight of stairs will have to rise from another room, and this

Good insulation is essential in any loft conversion to keep heat losses down

A loft conversion can provide working space away from domestic bustle

When planning loft windows, it is essential to think about their future cleaning and maintenance requirements. They should be top- or side-hung so that they can be cleaned from inside, and the frames should be made from plastic or a durable hardwood.

If your loft has one or two gable ends, you could, of course, install windows in the gable-end walls. You are still likely to need additional windows in the roof's slope, however.

Apart from providing light and ventilation, the loft windows in a two-storey house must also allow a means of escape in the event of fire. The Building Regulations require an opening window that is at least 850mm (nearly 3ft) high and 500mm (about 18in) wide, with a sill placed between 600mm (about 2ft) and 1100mm (about 3½ft) above the loft's floor level, and at a maximum distance of 1700mm (5ft 7in) from the roof's eaves. These dimensions allow the use of a ladder for rescue purposes.

Insulating the loft's rooms

Loft rooms need good thermal insulation, which means lining their walls and ceilings with high-grade insulation products. The ceiling insulation must leave an air gap between this and the underside of the roof's slope, in order to allow ventilation and to prevent the formation of condensation in the insulation. Wall insulation can be provided by fitting insulation battens between the wall studs, and then lining the rooms with a thermal board containing a vapour barrier.

Preventing the spreading of fire

In the event of a house fire, you will also need to prevent the fire and smoke from spreading into the loft rooms from below. This involves fireproofing the stairwell, fitting self-closing devices to any doors that open on to the stairwell, and installing a fire door to the new loft room(s). The loft floor is also required to have a modified, 30-minute, fire-resistance standard, as well as interlinked, mains-powered smoke alarms on each floor of the house.

Providing services in the loft

You will certainly want an electricity supply in your new loft room, and also some form of space heating. If you plan to include washing and WC facilities, you may additionally need plumbing services.

Since there will already be light-circuit wiring at the loft's floor level, it is generally easy to extend it in order to provide lighting in the new loft rooms, as long as this does not cause the existing circuit to become overloaded. You may also be able to use spurs from an existing power circuit for supplying new socket outlets, but it is better to supply the loft from a new ring-main circuit, which will serve unlimited socket outlets. The loft's lighting can then be run as a fused spur from this circuit.

Heating can be provided by means of individual space heaters – storage heaters, for example – or you could extend the house's central heating system into the loft. There are several ways of doing this; consult a heating engineer for advice on the best solution for your circumstances.

If you want hot- and cold-water supplies in the loft room, there are again several available options. Perhaps the simplest is to install a mains-fed water heater in the loft; make it a combination boiler, and it can then supply the heating too. This will avoid the need for complex modifications to the existing plumbing and heating systems.

Getting rid of waste water from loft appliances is another consideration. Depending on the position of the existing soil stack, it may be possible to extend it and then run the loft room's waste pipes into it. Otherwise, to overcome the problems of over-long waste-pipe runs, a pumped macerator unit could be installed.

PLANNING THE WORK

Once you have established whether a loft conversion is a practical possibility, the next step is to plan the design in more detail, and to work out how to comply with the various rules and regulations concerned. It is essential, at this stage, to enlist some professional help in order to ensure that you do this, and also to make the best possible use of the space available for the conversion.

You could employ an architect or surveyor to advise you, either to produce plans for you or your builder to work from, or to supervise the whole project. Alternatively, you could leave the plans to your builder, if you are satisfied that he has experience of loft conversion work, or else you could call in one of the many specialist loft conversion companies, which will deliver the entire design, planning and construction package. Which route you choose will depend on the complexity of the project, and on whether you want to do some of the work yourself; you can certainly save a lot of money by arranging for your builder to do the main structural work, leaving the internal completion jobs to you, but few loft conversion specialists will agree to this level of flexibility.

DOING THE CONVERSION

Once the plans have been finalised, and approval has been granted, you have three choices regarding how to proceed.

If you have the time and the practical skills, you could carry out the entire conversion yourself. This will be the cheapest method by far, but is also likely to be the slowest. Think carefully about taking this route if you do not want the house to be in a state of complete chaos for months.

In order to speed up the work, you could call in a builder to carry out the major structural alterations, and then either do the internal finishing work yourself, or arrange for individual subcontractors to do it for you. This is likely to be more expensive than a do-it-yourself conversion, but at least has the considerable merit of getting the messy structural work completed fairly quickly.

The third, and most expensive, option is to hand the entire job over to someone else – either a loft conversion specialist or (through your architect) a local firm of builders who will operate under their supervision. This route has the obvious advantage of giving you a completed loft conversion in no more than a couple of weeks.

WHAT THE JOB INVOLVES

If you decide to do the work yourself, it is vital to plan the sequence of operations in detail before you start. The job will involve the following stages.

1 Creating temporary, but safe, access to the loft space from the floor below, so that you can carry out any necessary strengthening work to the existing loft's floor. Getting new beams into the loft through the house may pose problems, but one way around this is to make a small, temporary opening in the roof (which will eventually become one of the roof's windows), so that the beams can be brought in from scaffolding erected outside the building.

2 Removing and repositioning any roof support timbers required by your plans, in order to open up the roof space ready for internal partitioning.

3 Putting down the new loft floor so that you have a safe working platform on which to carry out the subsequent stages of the work. At the same time, you may need to re-site existing water tanks and pipe runs, and to begin extending the plumbing and electrical circuits into the loft space so that they can be sited in the floor's void.

4 Installing the roof's windows. Unless there is a sound reason for you to construct dormers, fitting proprietary roof windows in the plane of the roof's slope will be by far the quickest and neatest way in which to light your loft rooms, and the work can be entirely carried out from inside the roof. If there are gable walls in the loft, you could, of course, install windows in these, after fitting lintels with which to carry the load over the openings. This will then allow you to work in the loft by natural light.

5 Putting in the wall frames, and installing the insulation on the underside of the roof's slopes, while always maintaining good ventilation to the roof timbers.

6 Completing the running of the pipework and wiring to wherever it is required within the loft space, and then adding insulated wall cladding with which to form the rooms.

7 Constructing a new staircase to the loft from the storey below, and carrying out any necessary alterations to the existing stairwell in order to satisfy the fireproofing requirements of the Building Regulations.

8 Completing the fitting and decoration of the conversion.

Outbuildings

Outbuildings of one sort or another are popular additions to many gardens. Some, such as summerhouses, sauna cabins and swimming-pool enclosures, are built purely for the purpose of pleasure. Others – sheds and greenhouses, for example – have both work and leisure uses, or can be used as overflow storage spaces for items such as gardening tools and equipment, or outdoor furniture. Yet others provide homes for pets, and even livestock. Within reason, you can put up as many outbuildings as you like (but see Rules and regulations opposite).

As delightful an outhouse as you could imagine for storing garden furniture or over-wintering the barbecue

Timber, painted if you like, is the ideal choice for garden sheds and other small outbuildings

OPTIONS

Building from scratch

You can create outbuildings to your own design using masonry, timber, glass and sheet-roofing materials as appropriate, and this may be the best solution if you want to erect a building that is unusual in design or purpose. Building it yourself allows you to incorporate features such as good thermal insulation, extra security devices, a sturdy workbench or specialised storage space. Any structure that you build will need the appropriate foundations, and, if the building is of lightweight, timber-frame construction, you should take steps to ensure that it is securely fixed to the foundation slab so that high winds cannot shift it.

Using prefabricated buildings

There is such a wide range of prefabricated garden buildings available nowadays that most people will find what they want 'off the peg'. The majority of sheds, summerhouses and similar work and storage buildings are made in timber, but galvanised and factory-painted sheet-metal buildings are becoming more popular, while a few firms offer garden sheds and stores in the same pre-cast concrete panels that are used for kit garages. As a low-maintenance alternative to timber, aluminium is the ideal lightweight material for the framework of greenhouses, and plastic sheeting is now widely used instead of glass for glazing all sorts of garden buildings.

All prefabricated buildings come in a wide range of sizes, and are often designed on a modular basis, making it possible to increase the size of the building at a later date if you need more space simply by adding extra wall and roof sections.

As with self-built structures, prefabricated buildings need a solid base of some sort – a concrete slab for sheds and similar structures, and dwarf brick walls for greenhouses – to which the building can be securely anchored. Do not rely on just the building's weight to keep it in place: a strong gale could dislodge it. The manufacturers will provide specifications for the individual buildings in their range.

RULES AND REGULATIONS

Outbuildings do not need planning permission as long as:

♦ they are not put to any residential use

♦ they are not erected in front of the building line — the wall of the house facing the highway

♦ their height does not exceed 4m (13ft) if they have a ridged roof, or 3m (10ft) if the roof is flat

♦ their erection will not result in more than half of the garden being covered by buildings; any already present, including garages that are situated more than 5m (16ft) away from the house (which are themselves classed as outbuildings), must be taken into account.

You do not need Building Regulations approval for outbuildings either, as long as the building does not exceed 30sq m (325sq ft) in area, and is either built from non-combustible material, or is situated at least 1m (3ft 3in) from the property's boundary.

Separate swimming-pools (as opposed to any buildings housing them) need approval from your local water supply company, and installing one is likely to result in a marked increase in your water rates. (See pages 166–7 for more details.)

Plumbing

Unless you live in a new house, your plumbing system will almost certainly have been extended and modified over the years as new or additional facilities have been added to the system. Such additions and alterations may have been carried out professionally, but many homes suffer from a chaotic assortment of amateurish plumbing work that is frequently prone to leaks, poor rates of flow and other problems. These often become apparent during improvement work to kitchens and bathrooms, and such work can provide a golden opportunity to reorganise and replace the old pipework.

Fitting a new hot water cylinder is a job that many home-owners prefer to leave to a plumber

part from the pipework itself, other components of old systems, such as storage tanks and hot water cylinders, may be old-fashioned and n dire need of replacement. Changing these may lso provide an ideal opportunity to modernise various parts of the plumbing system.

In an old property, the original plumbing system vill have been run with lead or iron pipework; any nore modern additions will have been made in copper or even plastic pipework. Old pipework is likely o be seriously furred up in hard water areas, causing educed rates of flow, while lead pipes in soft water reas can pose a serious health risk. In such cases, ipping out all the old pipework and replacing it with nodern, non-toxic plumbing materials is the only afe solution to the problem.

OPTIONS

Replacing pipework

f you are planning an extensive replacement or eorganisation of your plumbing system, you will probably automatically think of using copper pipe. This is still the plumbing industry's standard material, and has the advantage of being both widely available and relatively inexpensive.

Plastic pipe is an alternative to copper if ease of use is more important than cost. It can be used for ot and cold water supplies, and also for central heating, as long as the first length of pipe next to the boiler is made of copper.

Rigid cPVC pipe is joined together with special solvent-welded fittings, while semi-flexible polybutylene and cross-linked polythene pipes can be connected with plastic push-fit fittings, or with standard brass compression fittings. The two semi-flexible types are sold in coils as well as in cut lengths, and can be bent round gentle 90° curves using special formers, thus cutting down on the number of fittings required when making up pipe runs.

If you are replumbing an old property with copper pipes, you will have to replace the galvanised water cisterns and tanks in order to eliminate the risk of electrolytic corrosion taking place between the two different metals.

If you are using plastic pipework to replace metal pipes, you must ensure that any metal fittings in kitchens and bathrooms are properly bonded to earth by running separate earth wires from these back to the main earth terminal in the house's consumer unit. Get an electrician to check the earth bonding if you do not know how to do this properly and safely.

Fitting thermostatic valves to your radiators will give you far better control of individual room temperatures

Replacing a cistern

If you have a galvanised iron water storage cistern, it will probably be suffering from corrosion, and is likely to spring a leak at any time. Replacing it with a plastic cistern will overcome this problem, and will give you a cold water storage facility that meets the requirements of the current water bye-laws.

Rigid plastic cisterns are made in a range of sizes, but it can be difficult to get a large cistern through a small loft hatch. If this is a problem, you could either install two smaller interconnected cisterns, or fit a circular flexible type, which can then be deformed so that it can be passed through the loft's hatch.

All new cisterns have to meet the requirements of Water Bye-law 30, and should be sold with a kit of accessories with which to ensure compliance. This kit includes a cover, an insulating jacket, a screened breather pipe, an overflow-pipe connector with an insect filter and internal dip tube, a grommet for making the vent-pipe connection and a metal plate for supporting the ball-valve connection.

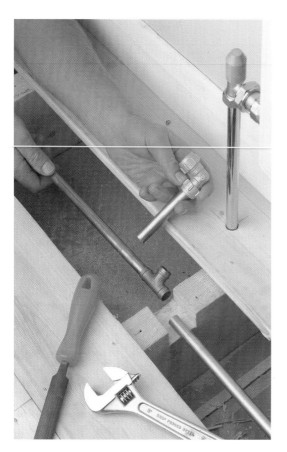

Replacing a hot water cylinder

There are several reasons why you might want to fit a new hot water storage tank: the existing one may be an old galvanised iron type; you may have a direct cylinder that you want to convert to indirect operation; or your indirect cylinder may be badly furred up as a result of hard water scale. You may also simply have a leaky cylinder.

If you are replacing an existing copper cylinder, you should be able to find a replacement of the same size as the original, although the pipework connections are unlikely to match exactly, and some modifications will be needed before you can fit it. If you have an old galvanised tank, the main problem will probably be disconnecting the pipework from it; cutting the pipes and remaking the connections to the new cylinder is generally the quickest solution.

Fitting an unvented hot water system

If you have a traditional hot water system that includes a cold water storage tank and a hot water

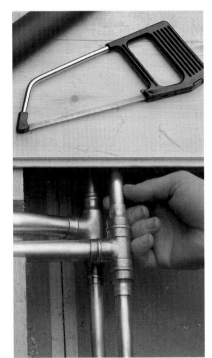
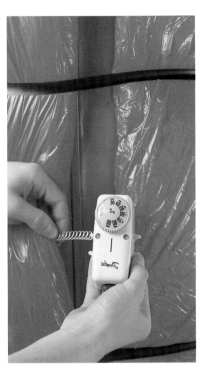

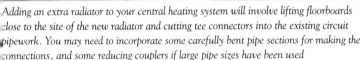
Adding an extra radiator to your central heating system will involve lifting floorboards close to the site of the new radiator and cutting tee connectors into the existing circuit pipework. You may need to incorporate some carefully bent pipe sections for making the connections, and some reducing couplers if large pipe sizes have been used

Adding a cylinder thermostat to your hot water cylinder will help prevent wasteful operation of the boiler. It is wired into the heating controls junction box

cylinder, and both need replacing, it is worth considering installing an unvented hot water system in their place.

With such a system, all the household's water – hot and cold – is supplied directly from the mains, which means that there is no need for a cold water storage tank. In this case, you can simply disconnect and abandon an existing storage tank in the loft, along with its attendant pipework, and never have to worry about frozen pipes again. Other advantages of unvented systems include no longer hearing a noisy cistern filling via a ball valve, having drinking water at all cold taps, getting equal water pressure at all outlets (which is especially useful for showers), and having no restrictions on where you place the hot water cylinder.

An unvented system incorporates a number of components designed to ensure its safe operation. These include:
♦ a line-strainer for removing particles from the water supply which could adversely affect the safe continuous operation of any valves on the system
♦ a pressure-reducing valve which ensures that the mains pressure does not exceed a safe level
♦ a non-return (check) valve which prevents hot water returning to mix with the cold water in the mains supply
♦ an expansion vessel that copes with the increase in volume of the water in the system as it heats up
♦ an expansion relief valve that allows expanding water to escape to the drains if the expansion vessel fails for any reason
♦ a special cylinder fitted with a thermostat, an energy cut-out device which turns off the boiler if the water temperature rises to 90°C, and a pressure-relief valve which discharges water to the drains if the temperature reaches 95°C.

Unvented hot water systems have to comply with Building Regulations requirements, as well as with the water bye-laws, and so must be fitted only by an approved installer. Your local authority should have details of such installers working in your area.

Porches

There are several advantages to having a porch: it provides shelter from the weather for callers while you answer the door, it is somewhere to leave wet shoes and umbrellas on rainy days, it is a refuge for the family pet, and acts as a useful airlock in winter between the warm house and the cold outdoors. If it is large enough, it can be used as a safe parking place for bikes and prams. It can even improve the appearance of your house, not to mention its security.

Careful attention to detail results in a porch that looks part of the original house

A front door set back in a recess to create a covered porch is a feature of many Victorian and Edwardian homes, and this style found favour again in the classic semi-detached house of the 1930s, in which a deep, enclosed porch was the sign of a status not enjoyed by cheaper, terraced homes with their simple canopies. Now external porches are back in vogue, whether they are built as part of a new house or are added to an existing one.

Porches do not generally require planning permission except in certain circumstances, and are exempt from Building Regulations control unless they exceed 30sq m (325sq ft) in area.

OPTIONS

If no porch exists

If your front door lies flush with the house wall, and you do not even have a canopy over it, an add-on porch is an obvious solution. The only restriction is whether you have the available space; you could have a porch of some sort with as little as a metre or so in front of the door, although in such a tight space you will almost certainly need to apply for planning permission (see box).

You have two main choices: to build an open porch – a canopy with side walls – or to erect a fully enclosed structure with a separate door, and possibly windows as well. The former option will be cheaper, but does not have the advantages of an enclosed porch, including – especially – the airlock effect. An enclosed type is generally a better choice, unless there are site restrictions such as the need to maintain access to the back garden past a porch sited at the side of the house.

If a canopy exists

If your house already has a canopy (either flat or pitched and tiled) over the front door, you can often use this as the basis for the construction of a fully enclosed porch. This will involve infilling the space between the ground level and the canopy; you will also have to lay a foundation slab to match the extent of the canopy, unless the existing doorstep is large enough to act as such. The actual construction work will be quite straightforward, whether the porch is part-brick and part-timber, or a fully glazed enclosure. All that you have to ensure is that the infilling material is securely fixed to the existing house wall and the canopy, and that the structure is damp-proofed; an existing ground slab will not incorporate a damp-proof membrane, and any new brickwork that bridges the house's dampcourse must incorporate a vertical dampcourse to prevent moisture from being transmitted into the house walls.

If a front bay window exists

If your house has a projecting single-storey bay window alongside the front door, it is worth considering extending the roof of the bay so that it can act as a canopy across the front door, and then infilling the area beneath the new canopy to create an enclosed porch. This option not only provides a reasonably sized porch, but also ensures that the structure will be in keeping with the design of the house.

If a recessed porch exists

If your house has a deeply recessed front door, you can easily create an enclosed porch by filling the front of the recess with a tailor-made frame containing an outer door and, if space permits, glazed side and top lights. In this case, echoing the existing sill lines and using timber of the same size as the house's windows will help to maintain the visual integrity of the design. As with a freestanding porch, you may prefer to move the existing front door to the outside – especially if it is the original, and so in perfect harmony with the look of the house – and then fitting a new, glazed door leading from the porch to the hall.

Building a porch

How you create your porch is a matter of personal choice. As far as the design is concerned, your primary aim should be to build something that is in keeping with the style of the house. Try to use similar materials to those used on the house's façade, copying masonry or rendering, cladding or tiles as appropriate, and also adopting the same door and window styles. You may be able to use your existing front door as the porch's door, replacing it with a plain or glazed inner door. As for the roof, copying

Even a simple canopy can be an attractive feature, adding interest to a bland façade

the style of the house's roof is the safest option, and a ridged or monopitch tiled roof is far more attractive than a flat one.

A useful guide to style is to look around your neighbourhood and see what has been done to houses similar to your own.

Most people opt for a custom-built porch, either erecting it themselves, or employing a local builder to do so for them. One popular, and relatively inexpensive, solution is to use off-the-shelf window and door frames for forming the porch's walls; you merely have to connect them within a simple framework and then add the roof's structure. Alternatively, there are several firms that offer ready-to-assemble kit porches in modular form.

Whichever type you choose, there are two important points to remember. First, you will need proper foundations, even for a lightweight, all-timber structure. A concrete slab is usually sufficient for this, and can do double duty as the porch's floor, once a damp-proof membrane has been incorporated into it. Secondly, you must include a vertical dampcourse between the porch and the house walls, and you must also pay particular attention to waterproofing the joints between the porch and the house, both down the sides and at roof level.

Once the porch's structure is complete, make sure that it is secure, that the door has been sealed with draught strips, and that the porch's roof has its own guttering and downpipe. Finally, add a porch light, and make sure that the name or number of your house is clearly visible.

RULES AND REGULATIONS

Porches are exempt from Building Regulations control except in the unlikely event that they exceed 30sq m (325sq ft) in floor area. However, you will need approval if the porch also contains a WC compartment or a fuel store, or if it encloses a ventilation opening in the house's wall, or is built over an existing drain run.

As far as planning permission is concerned, a porch counts as permitted development in England and Wales as long as:

♦ its floor area does not exceed 3sq m (32sq ft)
♦ it is not more than 3m (about 10ft) in height
♦ it is at least 2m (6ft 6in) from any boundary situated between your property and a road or public footpath.

If you live in a conservation area, or if your house is a listed building, you must apply for consent in order to build any type of porch. In Scotland, porches always need planning permission.

Replacement windows

As every home-owner knows, windows do not last for ever. Wood rots, metal rusts, putty crumbles, hinges sag. As a result, the rain seeps in, and draughts whistle round ill-fitting casements and sashes that stick firmly shut whenever you want to open them, and then refuse to close properly again. If this sounds familiar, it is time to consider having replacement windows fitted. Explore all the options before going ahead, however – the job can be a very expensive one.

A sympathetic choice of style and materials for these windows helps to unify the appearance of a much-altered property

The window replacement business is now a major sector of the home improvement market. A number of large firms operate nationally, and every area has a number of smaller local companies. All offer a considerable variety of products at a wide range of prices, and deciding which to choose can be a difficult decision – and an expensive one, if you get it wrong.

OPTIONS

Saving your existing windows

Before you start touring showrooms and collecting brochures, inspect your existing windows. They may not be in as bad a state as they look: a modicum of maintenance work may give them a new lease of life and may save you a great deal of money. In addition, replacing every window in the house will cost several thousand pounds, while dealing with the replacement in phases will place far less strain on your financial resources.

If some of your windows seem to have some use left in them, it will be worth replacing putty, squaring up and re-hanging sagging casements, and, if the frames themselves are still reasonably sound, even replacing rotten casements, sashes and opening top lights completely.

If, however, your windows really are past saving, and replacement is the only viable option, you have several possible courses of action.

Replacing like with like

You can fit new windows of a similar type and style to those that you are replacing. A wide variety of windows made from wood, steel and aluminium is available from builders' merchants, timber yards, and some DIY superstores, sold in a range of traditional standard patterns and sizes. You could either do the actual replacement work yourself, or else call in a local builder to do it for you.

This is the least expensive replacement option, but may leave you with thermally inefficient single glazing, and the prospect of a future recurrence of your existing maintenance problems.

Choosing high-performance windows

The second route that you could take is to choose high-performance replacement windows that combine the most up-to-date design and construction techniques with materials that promise minimal future maintenance, and which have the additional benefit of including sealed-unit double glazing and

A little regular maintenance will help prolong the life of ageing windows for a few more years

Accurate measuring is essential when ordering replacement windows that you intend to install yourself

built-in weatherstripping. The only difficulty that you might experience is in finding windows that match the architectural style of your home, but window manufacturers have come a long way since they produced the aluminium-framed picture windows that disfigured so many homes in the early days of the replacement window boom. Choosing high-performance windows will be an expensive option, but it will, in theory at least, ensure that your new windows are the best that money can buy.

Some window manufacturers will supply made-to-measure timber and uPVC windows for you to fit yourself, and if you are able to tackle the work involved in installing them you will make considerable savings when compared with the cost of employing a specialist firm to supply and fit the windows.

Single or double glazing?

All replacement window specialists offer windows that include sealed-unit double glazing as standard, but many off-the-shelf replacement windows supplied by outlets such as timber merchants are only designed to be single glazed.

It is vital when replacing windows in older houses to match them to the style of the property

The main advantages of double glazing are:
♦ the elimination of unpleasant cold down-draughts, which will allow you to make better use of your living space in winter
♦ a reduction of almost 50 per cent in the amount of heat lost through your window area, resulting in probable savings of around 10 per cent on your current heating bill
♦ less condensation on your windows, since the inner pane is not in contact with the outside air and is therefore much warmer than single glazing
♦ improved sound insulation, although this is due as much to better draught-stripping as to the double glazing; if noise is a serious problem, you would do better to consider acoustic double glazing, which has a much wider air gap than that available in sealed units. (See Sound insulation on pages 160–1 for more details.)

With all these benefits, there is clearly little point in planning to install replacement windows that are not double glazed. The extra cost is not that high, especially when you consider that you would anyway have to buy glass for single glazed windows.

Frame materials

Two materials are nowadays commonly used for the frames of high-performance replacement windows: timber, and plastic (unplasticised polyvinyl chloride or uPVC for short).

Timber windows are either made from preservative-treated softwood, or from a rot-resistant hardwood, such as mahogany. Many have specifications

hat include integral weatherstripping and sealed-unit double glazing. Their main advantages are that:
• wood is an excellent insulator, so timber frames are warm and free from condensation
• they are readily available in a very wide range of standard sizes and styles, and can also easily be made to measure
• they are generally the cheapest type of replacement window frame
• they can be painted or stained quickly and easily in any colour you want.

The need for routine maintenance must be set against these advantages, however. Softwood windows need regular redecoration in order to keep rot at bay, and hardwood types require occasional treatment with preservative stain if they are to be kept in good condition.

Plastic windows incorporate steel or aluminium internal cores for extra strength, and, because of their relatively large variety of stiles and rails, they make ideal replacements for many older-style timber windows. Their main advantages are that:
• their frame members are good insulators
• they need virtually no maintenance
• they come in numerous styles, and some are available in coloured and wood-grain finishes, as well as in plain white.

The one drawback to plastic windows is that it is difficult to fit additional security devices to them, so it is important to check that good locks have been fitted as standard.

There is now a new British Standard Kite-mark scheme for improved security windows, which are designed to pass rigorous tests of strength. Such windows are worth looking for if good security is of prime importance to you.

Whichever type of window you choose, make sure that it has at least one casement or sash that can be easily opened, in order to provide an escape route in the event of fire or any other emergency.

Frame styles

The importance of choosing replacement windows that suit your house cannot be stressed enough: the appearance of many houses has been ruined, as far as their architectural style is concerned, by the addition of unsuitable new windows.

Thankfully, windows now come in a multitude of styles, enabling you to choose windows with conventional casements and top lights, or with top-hung, pivoting and tilt-and-turn panes. You can also buy double glazed, vertical-sliding sash windows,

These new windows have destroyed the look of this row of terraced houses

Many local joinery firms will make one-off replacement windows to match existing ones

which means that matching the existing style of your house with that of its neighbours should no longer be a problem.

The type of glass that is fitted into the window also comes into the 'looks' category. Most replacement windows are fitted with clear glass, but you could also choose obscured, patterned or coloured glass, although these options are usually available only by special order.

Equally important is the use of safety glass in vulnerable areas such as low-level glazing. The use of solar-control and low-emissivity glass, both of which help to retain heat inside in winter and to prevent rooms overheating in summer, is also increasing. Ask your windows supplier for advice about using these as an alternative to standard glass.

As an alternative to plain glass, you could also select sealed units that give your windows the small-paned Georgian look, or the appearance of leaded lights in square or diamond formats.

Rewiring

Many wiring systems are unable to deliver the service to homes that modern living standards demand. Lighting is often inadequate and old-fashioned, and power circuits do not provide enough socket outlets for all the appliances that we want to use. The solution is to rewire the house completely to modern standards. There is no reason why you should not carry out this task yourself so long as you are a careful and competent worker and you fully understand what you are doing. Since the work is very labour-intensive, you could then spend the money saved by installing better-quality fixtures and fittings. Even if you prefer to employ a professional electrician to do the job for you, you should still be closely involved in planning the system that you want.

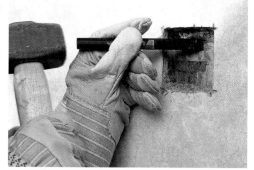

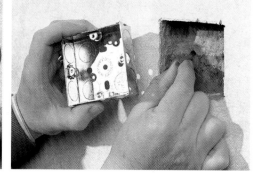

Flush-mounted wiring accessories always look neater than surface-mounted ones. Installing them in a masonry wall involves the following steps (left to right, top to bottom).
1 Hold the mounting box in place and check that it is level. Then draw round it with a pencil 2 Use a club hammer and cold chisel to chop out the masonry to the required depth, and test-fit the box 3 Cut a chase for the cable up or down the wall 4 Drill and plug fixing holes in the recess and screw the box in place. Run cable to it in conduit 5 Connect up the accessory and screw it to the box

*T*he best way of planning is to draw up some floor plans: one for upstairs and one for downstairs. They do not need to be architecturally accurate, but it helps to draw them roughly to scale so that you can use them to help to estimate the quantities of cable needed for the various circuits. Then make copies of each plan, so that you can plan the lighting and power circuits at each level of the house separately.

ASSESSING YOUR NEEDS

Your first step should be to decide exactly what sort of electrical services you need in each room in the house. Begin with the lighting, using one set of floor plans for the ground-floor rooms, and a second for those upstairs. The usual minimum provision in every room is a single lighting point in the centre of the ceiling, but this is not essential, and you can dispense with it if you intend to provide lighting by other means – for example, with wall lights, perimeter lighting or fittings recessed into the ceiling or concealed above kitchen worktops.

As you move from room to room, mark on your plan the positions of your chosen individual lighting points, and where you will want to site the switches for controlling them. You can, of course, control a light from more than one switch, which is useful in stairwells and long corridors, as well as in living-rooms and bedrooms where you may want to turn a light on at one switch and off at another. Remember also to include lights in utility areas such as lofts and walk-in cupboards.

Think about outside lighting too, both on the house's walls and further away from the building. Sockets very near the house can be supplied from the indoor circuits, but ones further away must have a separate circuit.

Repeat this exercise on another set of plans for the power circuits at each level of the house. Start by pinpointing the positions of the socket outlets and fused connection units that will serve individual appliances. Always specify double outlets unless there is a good reason for installing a single one at a particular location. Think about the level at which each outlet will be installed; many will be mounted just above skirting-board level, but there are several situations in which a higher position would be more appropriate. In kitchens, plan to include single, unswitched outlets in all the appliance recesses, which are controlled by double-pole switches fitted above worktop level.

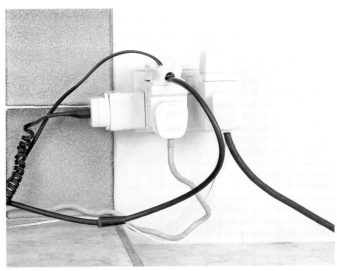

Never overload socket outlets with adaptors. Fit more outlets instead

When you have planned the positions of the socket circuits, mark in the connection points for individual, heavy current users, such as the cooker, the immersion heater, an instantaneous shower or night storage heaters.

Finally, think about outside power supplies, either in outbuildings or in the garden. You can now begin to work out how this assessment of your needs will translate into individual circuits, and start to produce a detailed list of all the components that you will need for the job.

PLANNING THE NEW CIRCUITS

Tackle the lighting circuits first. These are now rated at 6 amps, and can, in theory, supply up to 13 lighting points, each rated at a nominal 100 watts. In practice, you should restrict each circuit to the supply of no more than about eight points, thus allowing for the use of high-wattage lamps, or of several lamps per fitting. Each circuit will usually run from point to point, terminating at the most remote fitting on the circuit. Two lighting circuits will suffice in most homes – one for upstairs and one for downstairs – but you could give the living-room its own circuit if it will have a high lighting demand. You can wire any outside lights on the house's wall into one of the house's lighting circuits, but lights that are installed far away from the house must have their own separate circuit.

Next, plan the socket outlet circuits. These are wired as 32-amp ring circuits, and a typical home

Wire outside lights on the house's wall into one of the house's lighting circuits

will need two. However, since modern kitchens contain several appliances with high current demands, it is a good idea to allocate one ring circuit to the kitchen alone, one to other downstairs rooms and one for upstairs. Each circuit can serve rooms with a total floor area of 100sq m (1,075sq ft), and can include an unlimited number of outlets. The circuit cable runs from the fuseway in the consumer unit to each socket in turn, before returning to the same fuseway; spurs from the circuit can supply any outlets that are some distance from the main ring route. If you want to supply power outside, you will need a separate radial power circuit, rated at 20 amps.

You should now know how many lighting and power circuits your house will need. Add to these the individual circuits needed for a cooker (provide one even if you cook with gas), an immersion heater, an electric shower, and possibly 6-amp circuits for a burglar alarm and interconnected, mains-powered smoke detectors, in order to calculate the total number of separate circuits required. Add up the total load, and then check with your electricity supply company that your service cable and main cut-out fuse are large enough to cope with the demand.

THE CONSUMER UNIT

You should now choose a consumer unit that has sufficient fuseways for your needs. You should allow for a few spare fuseways, so that any future extensions to the house wiring system can be made with the minimum of inconvenience and disruption.

Always specify a unit containing miniature circuit breakers (mcbs), instead of fuses, with which to provide individual circuit protection. These are much more convenient than fuses (if more expensive), and are more sensitive to overloading.

For vulnerable circuits, provide protection against the risks of shock or fire caused by electrical faults by adding a residual current device (RCD) in order to create a split-load consumer unit. The circuits which receive RCD protection should include all ring circuits, circuits to cookers and showers, and those supplying equipment used outside. Other circuits – for lighting, burglar alarms and so on – will be controlled by the unit's main on/off isolator switch.

PLANNING CIRCUIT LAYOUTS

You have two choices of method when it comes to rewiring a house. The first is to follow tradition, and to conceal cables beneath floors and within wall chases, but this will involve a considerable degree of upheaval, as fitted floor coverings will have to be lifted, and wall decorations can be damaged. The other option is to use modern, surface-mounted cable-trunking systems for carrying the cables to switches, socket outlets and other power accessories. The trunking replaces skirting boards, architraves and cornices, and allows you to reach everywhere except to ceiling-mounted lighting points (these can be supplied by surface-mounted mini-trunking systems, or can simply be dispensed with altogether if other types of lighting are used).

Whichever method you prefer, you can now draw on your plans the positions of the cable runs for all the circuits, and use the scale to which your plans have been drawn to estimate approximately how much cable you will need for each circuit. For the sake of economy, since you will be using a lot of both types, aim to buy the cable for the lighting and ring circuits on 50m (about 165ft) or 100m (about 330ft) drums, and to buy the other cable sizes that you will need by the metre.

DOING THE WORK

If you decide to carry out the work yourself, it is essential to split the work into manageable stages. If you have a typical two-storey house, divide the job into three stages, as follows:

♦ ground-floor level – the downstairs power circuits

Good lighting in the bathroom is essential. These make-up lights are set in splashproof lampholders for safety

◆ first-floor level – the downstairs lighting circuits and upstairs power circuits
◆ loft level – the upstairs lighting circuits.

Throughout the job, leave the existing wiring undisturbed and install the new system alongside it. Once the new system is in place and is connected to the new consumer unit, you can then disconnect and remove the old wiring accessories and their mounting boxes, cut back and abandon the old cables, and tidy everything up. All that then remains is to call in an electrician or your electricity supply company to test the installation, issue a test certificate, and switch over the supply and earth connections to the new consumer unit. Under no circumstances should you ever attempt to make these connections yourself.

SAFE WIRING IN THE BATHROOM

Remember that you are not allowed to fit socket outlets in bathrooms, except for special shaver supply units or striplights containing a transformer. To provide power for wall heaters and towel rails, use fused spurs from the upstairs ring circuit. For a wall heater with its own switch, simply run cable from the fused connection unit to the heater. For appliances without switches, run cable from the connection unit to a ceiling-mounted cord-operated switch, then on to a flex outlet next to the appliance. Wire the appliance to the flex outlet with three-core flex. Make sure that all exposed metal in the room is safely cross-bonded to earth with 2.5mm² sheathed earth cable.

Sound insulation

Noise is, without doubt, the biggest source of nuisance in many people's lives, whether it is produced by traffic, aircraft, nearby factories or thoughtless neighbours. The noise itself is annoying enough, disturbing sleep and fraying nerves; worse still, persistent noise can be so disruptive that it can eventually lead to serious illness. If you live in an environment in which noise is a problem, you will need to install some form of sound insulation in your home.

Traffic noise can be greatly reduced by good sound insulation

To work out what type of insulation will help to reduce noise, you need to appreciate how sound travels from its source to your ears; it does so in one of two ways. The first is as airborne sound, which is transmitted as a series of pressure waves that travel through the air in much the same way as waves on water. When these waves strike something solid, they can either be reflected from it or absorbed by it, or they can make it vibrate and so transmit the sound onwards. Soft materials such as carpets and upholstery absorb sound, while hard surfaces such as plaster reflect it.

The most effective way to tackle airborne sound is to erect physical barriers between you and the sound's source; the denser the barriers, the more effective they will be. The barriers must also be uninterrupted for sound waves pass through any gaps.

The second way in which sound travels is as impact sound, which is generated when one object strikes another – for example, when something is dropped on the floor. The noise generated by impact sound may reach your ears directly, or may set up vibrations in the fabric of the building which, in turn, transmit the noise onwards. This effect is known as flanking transmission, and mass, once again, is the best way in which to prevent it. Older houses perform far better than modern, lightweight buildings in this respect.

The use of sound-absorbing materials can also help: for example, thick carpets and underlays will reduce the level of noise made by impacts such as heavy footfalls. Similarly, airborne noise such as music or speech can be deadened by the use of sound-absorbent wall and ceiling finishes in the room from which the noise originates, thus preventing it from creating vibrations in the room's structure that then transmit the noise onwards.

Improving sound insulation in the home means looking at each part of the house's structure in turn.

OPTIONS

Insulating windows

The weakest link in the outer envelope of your home is the windows. The first step to take in preventing external noise from entering the house is obviously to keep your windows closed, and to make sure that rooms receive adequate ventilation through alternative means that do not allow noise to enter from outside. Sound can penetrate the smallest gaps, which makes efficient draught-stripping important too.

If you want to achieve even better sound insulation, you should consider acoustic double glazing. Unlike double glazing used for keeping heat in, in which the optimum gap between the panes is about 20mm (just under an inch), acoustic double glazing needs a much wider air gap, of at least 100mm (about 4in) and ideally as much as 200mm (about 8in). In order to attain this, you will have to fit secondary double glazing as close to the inner edge of the window reveal as possible.

You can further improve the performance of acoustic double glazing by lining the sill, and the top and sides of the window reveal, with acoustic tiles.

Insulating doors

External doors can be almost as weak a part of the house's structure as the windows, especially if they are partly or fully glazed. To improve their sound insulation performance, you will need to apply the same principles as for windows. Fit draught-stripping round the sides and head of the door, and add a threshold excluder to close off any air gap underneath it. Even a letterbox opening can admit sound; fitting a hinged and draught-stripped flap on the inside will help to prevent noise entering the house by this route.

Doors with light plywood panels or hollow cores can be given both extra weight and sound insulation by the addition of plywood panels to the doors' faces. Alternatively, consider replacing them with solid timber doors, which, because of their greater weight, are better at preventing sound transmission.

Insulating walls

There is not a great deal that you can do to improve the performance of your house's walls as far as sound insulation is concerned. They are already the most efficient part of the building in absorbing sound, and the expense of trying to improve their sound insulating properties generally cannot be justified.

However, party walls between houses are worth insulating, as anyone who has lived in semi-detached or terraced accommodation will testify.

The most cost-effective solution is to erect an insulated stud-partition wall on your side of the party wall. In order to reduce flanking transmission, this must be constructed independent of the party wall – in other words, it must not touch it at any point.

Building such a wall will involve:

1 fitting head and sole plates to the ceiling and floor, just in front of the party wall
2 fitting vertical studs between the plates at 600mm (just under 2ft) intervals
3 suspending lengths of 100mm (about 4in) glass-fibre loft insulation material between the studs, using battens pinned to the head plate
4 lining the face of the partition with two layers of 13mm (about half an inch) plasterboard, staggering the joints between the two layers, and then taping and filling them
5 using mastic for sealing any gaps round the perimeter of the new wall.

This work will cause fairly major disruption, especially if it is carried out throughout the entire house,

but it is relatively inexpensive and will bring about a significant reduction in noise transmission.

Insulating floors

Within a single household, sound passing between floors is rarely a problem, but it can quickly become so in buildings that have been converted into flats.

The best way of improving the soundproofing from above is to create what is known as a 'floating' floor. This involves creating a new floor surface from the existing floor by means of a continuous layer of glass-fibre or mineral-wool quilt. The easiest way of doing this is to lay the quilt over the existing floorboards, and then to put a new chipboard or plywood floor deck over it. Fitting such a floor will mean having to shorten the existing doors and repositioning built-in furniture, and can cause problems of differing levels between rooms, unless all the rooms on the same floor are given floating floors.

Insulating ceilings

Ceiling insulation is most likely to be needed in those flats and conversions in which the problem is noise from the flat above. It is less disruptive to install than a floating floor, since you do not need access to the room above, and it will not significantly alter the room's proportions, unless it already has unusually low ceilings.

You can construct a floating ceiling by using a variation on the technique described earlier for soundproofing party walls. Start by suspending new ceiling joists across the room on hangers or wall plates. Lay a glass-fibre or mineral-wool quilt above the joists, then nail on a double skin of 13mm (about half an inch) plasterboard, with the joints staggered between the two layers. Tape and fill all the joints carefully, and seal the ceiling perimeter with mastic.

Staircases and landings

You probably regard your staircase as an integral part of the house, and it is certainly the most complex piece of joinery in the building. For this reason, few people contemplate replacing it unless they are extensively modifying the house's interior, or unless the staircase has been badly damaged over the years by misuse, lack of essential maintenance, or even attacks of dry rot or woodworm. However, a far simpler job to carry out is the replacement of an unfashionable or damaged handrail and balustrade.

A simple, tailor-made staircase in an all-wood setting

The one feature of the staircase that is often replaced is the guarding – the handrail and the balustrade beneath it that stop you falling off the landing or the open side of the flight of stairs. Tastes in interior design change, and over the years many old balustrades have been removed or boarded up, or have been replaced by once-fashionable alternatives, such as solid infills, horizontal planking or decorative wrought-iron panels. Today's fashion is to restore the traditional appearance by fitting turned balusters beneath a hardwood handrail, and, thanks to the arrival of easy-to-use prefabricated components, installing new guarding on an existing staircase is now a relatively simple job, requiring just basic woodworking skills.

OPTIONS

Replacing the flight

If your staircase has been severely neglected or damaged, you may prefer to replace it completely rather than to try to repair the damage. How easy this will be depends on the type of staircase.

The simplest staircase is a straight flight rising directly from the hall to the landing. Many flights, however, change direction as they rise, either by means of triangular steps called risers, or through intermediate landings that turn the flight through 90° or 180°. A quarter-turn flight turns through 90°, and has a square quarter-landing that is as wide as the flight itself; a half-turn, or dogleg, flight turns through 180°, and has a half-landing twice as wide. If there is a space between the two flights on a half-turn staircase, this is known as an open-well, or open-newel, flight.

The advantage of quarter-turn and half-turn staircases is that they occupy less ground-floor space than a straight flight, so can make it easier to replan the layout of the house. However, they are more expensive than a straight flight, and are more complicated to install.

Many staircases in old houses were built on site from scratch, but it is usually possible, with a little ingenuity, to adapt modern, prefabricated flights to serve as replacements for these. Standard widths are 864mm (34in) and 915mm (36in), and there are

In a living-room a stylish modern staircase can be the focal point

A dream open-well flight of stairs serves two floors in this large house

three common lengths, with six, twelve and fourteen treads (that is, with seven, thirteen and fifteen risers). The six-tread version is ideal for quarter-turn and half-turn flights, and the fourteen-tread length is essential for houses with high ceilings.

The main problem with modern replacements arises because the existing staircase was probably constructed before the introduction of the modern Building Regulations, and so may be steeper and have fewer treads than is now permitted. Fitting the new staircase will generally mean 'borrowing' floor space at the foot of the flight, in order to allow for the lower pitch of the flight, and the need to incorporate an extra tread.

If this approach is not possible, you have little alternative to commissioning a custom-built replacement from a local joiner or woodwork manufacturer, which will be expensive. Whatever type of staircase you install must meet the requirements of the Building Regulations (see below).

Replacing the guarding

If your staircase is sound but you want to replace the guarding, you can buy kits consisting of prefabricated parts – including newel posts, balusters, handrails and turning pieces, as well as all the necessary fixings – and tackle the job yourself. It involves:

1 removing the existing handrail and balustrade
2 cutting down the newel posts to the level of the staircase strings
3 attaching new newel posts to the stubs
4 fitting the new handrail between the newel posts
5 setting the new balusters in place between the string and handrail.

It is worth painting or staining the new balusters before making up the balustrade, so that once it is in position only some touching-up work will be needed.

Dealing with landings

You can use the same prefabricated stair handrail components to replace the guarding round your landing too and give the refurbished stairwell a completely coordinated look. Follow the same sequence of operations as that for removing the existing guarding (see above), attach the new newel posts, fit the handrail and set the new balusters in position. The only difference is that the balusters will have square-cut ends instead of angled ones. Remember that the same rules and regulations for staircases apply to guardings on landings as well.

Fitting a spiral staircase

If you are extending or remodelling your home, you might be tempted to consider installing a spiral staircase. Most types have a central pillar with slot-on brackets that support the open treads with a handrail round the outside of the spiral. Spiral staircases are sold as kits, and the standard components can be used to make up almost any configuration of staircase. Make sure that any spiral staircase you are considering buying conforms to the requirements of British Standard BS5395 part 2.

There are two important things to remember about spiral staircases. The first is that installing one will not generally save much space at ground-floor level; the only discernable advantage is that the space occupied by the staircase is more square than rectangular, which may make better use of the space on the floors that it links. The second point is that while spiral staircases can look attractive, they are neither very practical (especially for moving furniture between floors), nor very safe for small children or elderly people. They are also not practical as a fire-escape route, so if you must have one make sure that it is a secondary staircase supplemented by a conventional flight elsewhere in the house.

RULES AND REGULATIONS

The Building Regulations include a number of requirements for new and replacement staircases, some of which will also apply if you are only replacing the guarding.

♦ The angle of the flight (known as the pitch) must not exceed 42°.

♦ All the steps in the flight should have the same rise (tread height) of not more than 220mm (about 8in), and the same going (the horizontal distance between consecutive step nosings) of at least 220mm (about 8in). For any step, the sum of twice the rise plus the going must fall between 550mm (21in) and 700mm (27in).

♦ There must be 2m (about 6ft 6in) of clear headroom over the length and width of the flight above an imaginary line joining the steps' nosings.

♦ Open-tread stairs must be constructed so that a 100mm (about 4in) diameter sphere cannot pass between the treads, and adjacent treads should overlap by at least 16mm (about half an inch).

♦ On flights with tapered treads, the going should be measured at the centre of the tread, with the rise and going falling within the same limits as for a straight flight. The going must be at least 50mm (about 2in) at the narrower end of the tread.

♦ A handrail must be fitted at one side of flights less than 1m (3ft 3in) wide, and at both sides on wider flights. Each rail should be at least 900mm (about 35in) high.

♦ Balusters must be spaced so that a 100mm (about 4in) diameter sphere cannot pass between them, and their design should not enable children to climb the guarding.

♦ There must be a landing at the top and bottom of every flight, as wide and as long as the minimum width of the staircase.

♦ Where a door opens outwards on to a landing at the bottom of the flight, there must be a clear space across the full width of the flight of at least 400mm (about 16in) to avoid the risk of collisions between users.

Swimming-pools

Having a swimming-pool in your back garden is a permanent health and leisure centre on your own doorstep, to be enjoyed in privacy by family and friends, and is the perfect focal point for occasions such as parties and barbecues. A swimming-pool is also eminently affordable, and few home improvements can be relied upon to give so much pleasure to so many for so long. Having one could completely change your life, and it may also enhance the value of your home if you decide to sell. There are several types of swimming-pool from which to choose.

Finish off the pool surround with a hard, non-slip surface

OPTIONS

Above-ground pools

Above-ground pools are designed to be assembled from prefabricated components on any flat, level surface, and are the least expensive type available. The walls consist of ribbed-steel, or reinforced glass-fibre sections that are locked together and fitted with a heavy-duty, flexible, waterproof liner. They can usually be put up in a day, come in a range of shapes and sizes, and can even be taken with you when you move house.

They do have their drawbacks, however. Getting into above-ground pools can be difficult, especially for small children; you cannot dive into them; and, above all, they are fairly unattractive structures that are hard to camouflage successfully without resorting to extensive planting or landscaping.

Prefabricated in-ground pools

Somewhat more expensive are the variations on the above-ground type of pool, which are designed for installation in the ground. A wide range of shapes and sizes is again available, and the pool can be deep enough to allow diving. The necessary excavation work makes this type of installation a more expensive option, but it allows for much easier access to the pool, quite apart from helping the pool to blend better with the garden.

You can also buy one- and two-piece glass-fibre pools in a limited range of shapes and sizes. These are delivered ready to be placed in a prepared excavation site, making installation extremely quick, but their size requires excellent access to the site from the road. They are also comparatively expensive.

In-ground concrete pools

At the top end of the price range are in-ground, concrete pools. These are built on concrete foundations, using either interlocking wall panels or reinforced blockwork, and are lined with mosaic tiles, marblite, or similar materials, to give a permanent, waterproof finish. Their cost obviously depends on factors of size and site, but you are likely to have to pay roughly the same as for a new family car.

Open-air or under cover?

It is the height of luxury to have an 'indoor' pool: you can use it all year round, day or night, you will not have to worry about covering it at night, and it will cost less to heat than an outdoor pool. Nor do you have to go to the expense of erecting a traditional building round your pool, unless that is what you want. Otherwise, you could build a Scandinavian-style log cabin round the pool, or use the wall, door and roof components of a conservatory in order to create a light and airy enclosure. If you cannot opt for these, there are plenty of lightweight or inflatable enclosures which can be used instead.

PLANNING YOUR POOL

For most people, cost is clearly a limiting factor when deciding which sort of pool to install. Despite this, an in-ground pool is without doubt the best investment, since it will allow you to enjoy a full range of aquatic and poolside activities. Pick the biggest pool that you can afford (or that your site will allow); you need to provide around 10sq m (33 sq ft) of pool area for every user, in order to avoid over-crowding, so a family of four would need a 40sq m (about 130sq ft) pool – a rectangle measuring 8x5m (about 26x16ft), for example, or a circular pool about 7m (about 23ft) across. If you want to be able to dive in from the side, one end should be at least 2m (6ft 6in) deep.

For easy access, allow an area of level ground all round the pool that is at least 1m (3ft 3in) wide, and finish it with a smooth, hard, non-slip surface that is easy to keep clean. Do not border the pool with grass: it quickly gets slippery and muddy, and you will end up with grass cuttings in the pool every time you mow the lawn. If space permits, increase the width of the pool's surrounding area to provide spaces for sitting and sunbathing.

The main cost involved in running a swimming-pool is its heating, and this will depend on the water temperature, the length of the swimming season,

Building an in-ground pool is not a job for the faint-hearted

how well the pool is covered at night, the weather – if you have an outdoor pool – and the warmth of the enclosure if it is inside. You will also have to spend small, regular sums on chemicals.

POOL ACCESSORIES

There is more to maintaining a swimming-pool than just filling a hole in the ground with several thousand gallons of water. That water has to be kept clean and heated. Necessary maintenance equipment includes:

♦ a surface skimmer for collecting débris such as leaves that blow into the pool

♦ a filtration unit for removing fine particles of dirt from the water

♦ a pump for circulating the water through the skimmer and filtration unit

♦ heating equipment, which can be solar-powered (the most economical to run), electric (if your house's electricity supply can cope with the extra load), or gas- or oil-fired. Alternatively, you could link a heat-exchanger to your domestic heating system, if the boiler is big enough, or you could install a heat pump

♦ a pool cover (unless your pool has its own enclosure), in order to keep débris out and heat in

♦ cleaning equipment for keeping the sides, bottom and surrounds of the pool clean, and water-treatment chemicals for disinfecting the water, killing algae, and maintaining the correct pH level (a measure of the water's acidity or alkalinity)

♦ optional extras such as walk-in steps, diving boards and underwater lights.

RULES AND REGULATIONS

You do not generally need planning permission in order to install a swimming-pool, although permission may be needed if you are planning to build a large enclosure or to put up poolside buildings, especially if the project results in more than half of the garden being occupied by the pool and other buildings.

Pools themselves are not subject to Building Regulations control, nor are pool enclosures, unless the building has a floor area of over 30sq m (325sq ft). However, if you are building an in-ground pool, you should contact your local building control officer to ask for advice about ground conditions, and to check whether any underground services cross the proposed site of the excavation.

You must notify your local water supply company of your plans. Installing a pool is likely to lead to a substantial increase in your water rates.

Thermal insulation

Insulation is an unglamorous but nevertheless very important part of the structure of your house. It keeps you warm in winter and cool in summer, and also helps to stop any heat loss from your hot water system, as well as preventing cold pipes from freezing in frosty weather. Apart from increasing your comfort, good insulation will also save you money, so if yours is below standard (or non-existent), attending to it is a home improvement project that is well worth carrying out.

 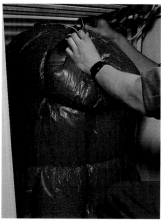

Wear gloves and a mask to lay a loft floor insulation blanket (left); and give your hot cylinder a jacket to keep the heat in (right)

OPTIONS

Pitched roofs

If you have a pitched roof, and you use the loft space only for storage, insulating the loft floor is one of the least expensive ways of improving your home's insulation. Unless you have a completely unmodernised property, there is already likely to be some insulation in the loft, but bringing it up to modern requirements will make a dramatic reduction in heat lost through the roof.

For this purpose you can use either blankets of glass fibre or mineral wool, which are sold by the roll, or loose-fill materials (vermiculite, a lightweight expanded mineral, is the most widely available). You can also have loose-fill insulation, usually mineral wool or fireproofed cellulose fibres, which is blown into your loft by specialist contractors.

Blanket materials tend to be easier to use than loose-fill types, unless your loft is awkwardly shaped, or has irregular joist spacings. The rolls are generally 400mm (about 18in) wide (to match the standard joist spacing), and common thicknesses are 100mm (about 4in) and 150mm (about 6in). Choose the latter, unless your loft already has a thin layer of insulation, and ensure that it is laid with special eaves baffles, in order to maintain adequate ventilation.

Apart from being awkward to handle, loose-fill materials have another drawback: to be as effective as the blanket types, they need to be laid to a greater depth – usually an extra 25mm (about 1in). Since few ceiling joists are deeper than 150mm (about 6in), this means that there is nothing to contain the insulation, unless you are prepared to fix battens to the top edge of every joist. Therefore, check your joist depth before using loose-fill materials.

When you have completely insulated the loft floor, secure a piece of insulation blanket to the top surface of the loft's hatch, and draughtproof the rebate into which it closes. Remember to insulate the cold water storage tank, the header tank that tops up your heating system, and also any exposed pipework within the loft. Leave the loft floor directly beneath the tanks uninsulated, so that a little warmth can reach them from below, and thus help to prevent them from freezing.

Flat roofs

You can insulate flat roofs in one of four ways. The first involves laying insulation above the existing roof deck, and then adding a new waterproof surface, so creating what the experts call a 'warm' deck. You can use either special composite insulation boards for this, complete with a bonded-on layer of roofing felt, or rigid insulation boards waterproofed with two layers of high-tensile roofing felt. In both cases, a solar-reflective finish should be applied to the roof's surface in order to reduce the effects of thermal stress, which can damage the felt.

The second method involves gaining access to the voids between the joists, either by removing the fascia boards outside or the ceiling inside, and then fitting an insulation blanket, or rigid insulation sheets, between the joists – this is known as a 'cold' deck. With this method, it is essential to leave an airspace 50mm (about 2in) deep between the top of the insulation and the underside of the roof deck, and also to provide ventilation holes on the opposite edges of the roof. This guarantees a crossflow of air through the airspace, so preventing condensation rotting the roof's timbers.

The third method is to create what is known as an 'inverted' warm deck, in which the insulation is placed above the roof's weatherproofing layer. This is normally done by laying special rigid insulation boards and a cement capping directly on to the roof deck; the advantage of this is that the weatherproofing layer remains close to room temperature all year round. However, thicker insulation is needed when compared with a warm deck.

The fourth method is to put up a false ceiling in the room below the flat roof, with insulation material and a vapour barrier sandwiched between it and the surface of the existing ceiling.

External walls

Your house's walls are the most massive part of the whole building, and absorb a lot of heat, which is why a cold house takes so long to warm up. You can retain this by insulating the walls in one of two ways.

The traditional cavity wall consists of two skins of masonry, with a gap – usually 50mm (about 2in) wide – between them. You can considerably improve their insulating performance by filling this cavity with insulating material. This process is carried out by specialist contractors who pump treated fibres, pellets or insulating foam into the cavity through holes drilled in the outer leaf of the wall. The type of insulation that you should choose depends chiefly on the degree of exposure to which your house is subjected, and your local building control officer will advise you on choosing both the correct material and an appropriate installer. Installing cavity wall insulation requires Building Regulations approval, and must be carried out only by approved installers. Note that cavity wall insulation is not suitable for timber-framed houses, which are already insulated.

If you have solid exterior walls, this option is not possible, and the most economical alternative is to dry-line them on the inside with insulating plasterboard, which is fixed directly to the wall with panel adhesive. Alternatively, you could secure standard, plasterboard sheets to wall battens, placing an insulation blanket or boards between the battens, and then covering them with a vapour barrier.

TANKS AND PIPES

Do not forget to insulate water storage tanks and pipework, especially when these are situated in cold areas such as insulated lofts. Tanks should be fitted with special plastic-covered insulation jackets, which are available in all standard tank sizes and shapes.

All pipework in the loft and below suspended timber ground floors should be insulated too, using proprietary foam pipe insulation. It is also worth insulating other pipe runs elsewhere in the house, even those carrying hot water, to cut heat losses.

Finally, fit an insulating jacket to your hot water cylinder, even if it already has shrunk-on foam insulation. Ready-to-fit jackets are available to suit all standard cylinder sizes.

Floors

Few people think of ground floors when considering insulation, yet a surprisingly large amount of heat can be lost through both direct-to-earth and suspended floors.

With suspended timber floors, you can fix insulation between the joists, after lifting the floorboards. You can either cut strips of rigid polystyrene insulation board and rest them on nails driven into the sides of the joists, or else suspend lengths of loft insulation blanket between the joists, using garden netting stapled over them to create 'hammocks' that will support the blanket.

With direct-to-earth concrete floors, the only practical method of insulation involves placing sheets of rigid polystyrene insulation directly on top of the floor's surface, and then putting down a new floating floor of tongued-and-grooved chipboard. This treatment will clearly require the lifting of built-in furniture, the replacement of skirting boards, and the shortening of room doors so that they clear the new raised floor.

Windows and doors

There are two steps that you can take in order to reduce heat lost through windows and doors. The first is to install some form of double glazing (see pages 96–7 for more details), or else to replace any existing windows and glazed doors with new ones containing sealed unit double glazing.

The second option open to you is to improve the draught stripping around external doors and opening windows. Remember that draught stripping eliminates many unofficial sources of ventilation, so effectively turning the house into a well-sealed box. Fuel-burning appliances such as boilers and room heaters must have an efficient source of ventilation if they are to burn efficiently and safely, so it would be wise to ask your fuel supplier to make certain that you have adequate ventilation in rooms that contain such appliances.

Walls

If the layout of your home no longer suits your family's requirements, you could change it by building or removing interior walls in order to create the required room layout. Subdividing large rooms by building timber-framed partition walls is a relatively simple job, although it may be made more complicated by the need to reposition services, and perhaps to insert an additional window in one of the new rooms. Creating a large through-room by removing a partition wall is also relatively straightforward if the wall is timber-framed, but if it is load-bearing a steel beam will have to be inserted in order to support the joists of the floor above. This is a job for which you may prefer to enlist professional help, and one which requires Building Regulations approval.

By removing a wall between two rooms you can create a dramatic feeling of space and light

OPTIONS

Creating a through-room

Removing an interior wall can help to give a cramped floor plan a far greater feeling of space and freedom of movement. Many people elect to knock the living- and dining-rooms together in order to create a large open plan living space, but you could just as easily combine the dining-room and kitchen, or the front living-room and entrance hall (but only if you have a separate porch). At the same time, you may be able to block up a now-redundant doorway, freeing an additional area of wall against which you can arrange your furniture and without detriment to the traffic flow.

The feasibility of the conversion depends on whether the wall in question is load-bearing or not. Although you can carry out some preliminary investigations yourself, it is wise to call in a builder or surveyor to assess the technical requirements and ensure that the conversion will be correctly carried out. It is not just a question of specifying the correct size of beam for the job, and ensuring that it has adequate bearings with which to carry the superimposed load: account must also be taken of the effect of any alterations on the stability of the flanking walls, and also on the foundations at each end of the wall that is being removed.

The job of removing a load-bearing wall will involve the following stages:

1 providing support for the ceiling joists that rest on the wall, and for any masonry situated above the position of the proposed beam. This can be done using adjustable steel props, or special prop-free wall supports that are inserted into slots cut above and below the position of the beam
2 cutting out the masonry along the line of the supporting beam
3 strengthening the masonry to enable it to support the ends of the beam by building reinforcing piers, or inserting bearer beams, in flanking walls
4 inserting the beam, jacking it up underneath the remaining masonry, and then placing mortared supporting pads beneath the beam's ends
5 encasing the beam in plasterboard in order to provide the necessary fire resistance
6 making good any disturbed plasterwork
7 removing the props once the supporting pads have hardened.

Partitioning a room

The other way to reorganise your floor plan is to sub-divide large rooms into two smaller ones. The most common conversions of this type are carried out in order to provide an extra bedroom, or to create an en suite bathroom within an existing room. Whatever you want to achieve, this task is much simpler than knocking rooms together; you can also generally build the necessary timber-framed partition walls in a day, although repositioning the radiators, light fittings, switches, and socket outlets on the new walls may take a little longer.

You must take care when providing access to the new rooms. Generally speaking, part of the available floor space will be taken up by providing a passage-way or lobby leading to the new room's door from the existing door's position, since giving access through an existing room is rarely a satisfactory solution.

It is also important to ensure that each new room has adequate natural light and ventilation. They are not allowed to share a window, and habitable rooms must have both an openable window and background trickle ventilation, which means that a new window may be needed in one of the rooms. Kitchens, utility rooms, bathrooms and WCs do not have to have a window, but they must have suitable mechanical ventilation. If a newly partitioned room contains a fuel-burning appliance, call in your fuel supplier to check that the room has adequate ventilation in order for the appliance to operate efficiently and safely.

Building a timber-framed partition wall involves:

1 establishing the best position for the wall
2 with suspended timber floors, checking that the sections of wall running parallel to the direction of the floor joists will stand directly over a joist, and providing supporting noggings between the joists if not
3 securing the new wall's head plate to the ceiling, if necessary after inserting noggings between the ceiling joists with which to hold the fixing screws
4 securing the wall's sole plate to the floor, vertically below the head plate
5 fixing vertical studs between the head and sole plates at 400mm (about 18in) or 600mm (just under 2ft) centres
6 creating door openings where necessary by cutting away the sole plate and lining the door's head and sides
7 fitting horizontal noggings between the studs in

The quickest way of dividing up a large room is to build a timber-framed partitioned wall

order to provide additional support for the cladding, and to act as fixing points for radiators, wall cupboards, and so on
8 running any wiring or pipework through the framework to the position where it is needed
9 placing insulation within the framework
10 cladding the wall with plasterboard, ideally using two layers with staggered joints in order to provide good sound insulation
11 taping and filling all the joints
12 completing the wiring work on the switches and socket outlets of the new wall, and connecting any radiators or sanitary ware
13 hanging new doors and fitting architraves
14 making good, adding skirting boards, and then decorating the new wall.

RULES AND REGULATIONS

Removing a load-bearing wall requires Building Regulations approval in order to ensure that the supporting beam is strong enough, is itself properly supported and fire-proofed, and that the structural integrity of the building will not be affected by the conversion work.

Partitioning an existing room must satisfy the requirements of the Building Regulations as far as the ventilation of the new rooms is concerned, and if either of the rooms will contain washing, bathing or WC facilities, the provision of new waste pipes also needs approval. You do not need to submit full plans, however. Instead, notify your building control officer of your intentions by submitting a building notice and any outline plans of the work involved, and he will arrange a site visit to check that the conversion complies with the rules.

You do not need planning permission if creating a through-room or partitioning an existing one, unless the conversion creates a change of use — for example, by providing a home office or a self-contained flatlet.

Addresses

Addresses appear below for all the organisations mentioned in the book with an asterisk by their names. In addition you will find here several other contacts that may prove useful in your home improvement projects.

ARCHITECTS AND SURVEYORS

Architects Registration Council 73 Hallam Street, London W1N 6EE
☎ 0171-580 5861

Association of Building Engineers Jubilee House, Billing Brook Road, Weston Favell, Northampton NN3 8NW
☎ (01604) 404121

Institute of Structural Engineers 11 Upper Belgrave Street, London SW1X 8BH
☎ 0171-235 4535

Royal Incorporation of Architects in Scotland (RIAS) 15 Rutland Square, Edinburgh EH1 2BE
☎ 0131-229 7205

Royal Institute of British Architects (RIBA) 66 Portland Place, London W1N 4AD
☎ 0171-580 5533

Royal Institute of Chartered Surveyors 12 Great George Street, London SW1P 3AD
☎ 0171-222 7000

Royal Society of Architects in Wales Midland Bank Chambers, 75A Llandennis Road, Cardiff CF2 6EE
☎ (01222) 762215

CONTRACTORS

British Decorators Association 32 Coton Road, Nuneaton CV11 5TW
☎ (01203) 353776

Building Employers Confederation 82 New Cavendish Street, London W1M 8AD
☎ 0171-580 5588

Council for the Registration of Gas Installers (CORGI) 4 Elmwood, Chineham Business Park, Crockford Lane, Basingstoke RG24 8WG ☎ (01256) 707060

Electrical Contractors Association (ECA) ESCA House, 34 Palace Court, London W2 4JG
☎ 0171-229 1266

Electrical Contractors Association of Scotland Bush House, Bush Estate, Midlothian EH26 0SB
☎ 0131-445 5577

Federation of Master Builders Gordon Fisher House, 14-15 Great James Street, London WC1N 3DP
☎ 0171-242 7583

Guild of Master Craftsmen 166 High Street, Lewes BN7 1XU ☎ (01273) 478449

Heating and Ventilating Contractors Association 34 Palace Court, London W2 4JG ☎ 0171-229 2488

Institute of Plumbing 64 Station Lane, Hornchurch RM12 6NB
☎ (01708) 472791

National Association of Plumbing, Heating and Mechanical Services Contractors 14-15 Ensign House, Ensign Business Centre, Westwood Way, Coventry CV4 8JA
☎ (01203) 470626

National Federation of Roofing Contractors 24 Weymouth Street, London W1N 4LX
☎ 0171-436 0387

National Inspection Council for Electrical Installation Contracting (NICEIC) Vintage House, 37 Albert Embankment, London SE1 7UJ ☎ 0171-582 7746

Scottish Decorators Federation 1 Grindlay Street Court, Edinburgh EH3 9AR
☎ 0131-221 1527

MATERIALS, SERVICES, MISCELLANEOUS

Arthritis Care 18 Stephenson Way, London NW1 2HD
☎ 0171-916 1500

Brick Development Association Woodside House, Winkfield, Windsor SL4 2DX
☎ (01344) 885651

British Bathroom Council Federation House, Station Road, Stoke-on-Trent ST4 2RT ☎ (01782) 747074

British Carpet Manufacturers Association 5 Portland Place, London W1N 3AA
☎ 0171-580 7155

British Cement Association Century House, Telford Avenue, Crowthorne RG35 6YS ☎ (01344) 762676

British Ceramic Tile Council Federation House, Station Road, Stoke-on-Trent ST4 2RT
☎ (01782) 747147

British Coatings Federation (paint) James House, Bridge Street, Leatherhead KT22 7EP ☎ (01372) 360660

British Ready Mixed Concrete Association (BRMCA) The Bury, Church Street, Chesham HP5 1JE
☎ (01494) 791050

British Red Cross Society (BRCS) 9 Grosvenor Crescent, London SW1X 7EJ
☎ 0171-235 5454

British Security Industry

Association Security House, Barbourne Road, Worcester WR1 1RS ☎ (01905) 21464

British Wood Preserving and Damp Proofing Association 6 The Office Village, 4 Romford Road, London E15 4EA ☎ 0181-519 2588

British Woodworking Federation 82 New Cavendish Street, London W1M 8AD
☎ 0171-872 8210

Building Research Establishment Advisory Service Bucknalls Lane, Garston, Watford WD2 7JR
☎ (01923) 664664

Chartered Institute of Arbitrators (CIArB) International Arbitration Centre, 24 Angel Gate, City Road, London EC1V 2RS
☎ 0171-837 4483

Conservatory Association 2nd Floor, Godwin House, George Street, Huntingdon PE18 6BU
☎ (01480) 458278

Disabled Living Foundation 380-384 Harrow Road, London W9 2HU
☎ 0171-289 6111

Draught Proofing Advisory Association PO Box 12, Haslemere GU27 3AH
☎ (01428) 654011

External Wall Insulation Association and National Cavity Insulation Association (as for Draught Proofing Advisory Association)

Glass and Glazing Federation 44-48 Borough High Street, London SE1 1XB
☎ 0171-403 7177

Guarantee Protection Trust 27 London Road, High Wycombe HP11 1BW
☎ (01494) 447049

Hire Association Europe

Glossary

722 College Road, Erdington, Birmingham B44 0AJ
☎ 0121-377 7707

Independent Warranty Association 21 Albion Place, Northampton NN1 1UD
☎ (01604) 604511

Institution of Electrical Engineers (IEE Wiring Regulations) Savoy Place, London WC2R 0BL
☎ 0171-240 1871

Kitchen Specialists Association PO Box 311, Worcester WR1 1ND
☎ (01905) 726066

Master Locksmiths Association Units 4-5, Woodford Halse Business Park, Great Central Way, Woodford Halse, Daventry NN11 3PZ
☎ (01327) 262255

National Association of Chimney Sweeps (NACS) St Marys Chambers, 19 Station Road, Stone ST15 8JP ☎ (01785) 811732

Royal National Institute for the Blind (RNIB) 224 Great Portland Street, London W1N 6AA
☎ 0171-388 1266

Royal National Institute for Deaf People (RNID) 19-23 Featherstone Street, London EC1Y 8SL ☎ 0171-296 8000

Timber Research and Development Association (TRADA) Chiltern House, Stocking Lane, Hughenden Valley, High Wycombe HP14 4ND ☎ (01494) 563091

Water Research Centre (water bye-laws) Fern Close, Pen-y-fan Industrial Estate, Oakdale NP1 4EH ☎ (01495) 248454

Wood Panel Industries Federation 265 Borrowby Road, Grantham NG31 8NR
☎ (01476) 63707

Aggregate Sand or gravel added to cement and water to make mortar and concrete. All-in aggregate is mixed sand and gravel.

Back boiler A boiler fitted behind a room heater in a fireplace recess, fired by gas or solid fuel. Back boilers must have a conventional flue.

Balanced flue A specially designed boiler flue that passes through an outside wall. The flue supplies air to the boiler as well as carrying away the combustion gases.

Baluster A decorative vertical post used beneath a handrail to make up a balustrade on staircases and landings.

Ballvalve A float-operated valve fitted in storage and WC cisterns to refill the cistern automatically when water is drawn from them.

Bargeboard Timber or synthetic board used to finish off the roof edge at gable ends.

Batt A semi-rigid slab of insulating material used inside cavity walls and for other thermal insulating jobs.

Casement window A window with side-hung casements and top-hung opening lights, plus a number of fixed panes.

Chase A channel cut in a masonry wall to allow pipework or electrical cables to be concealed beneath the wall surface.

Combination boiler A boiler which provides central heating and hot water, the latter on demand. It does away with the need for a hot water cylinder.

Consumer unit The control panel for a domestic electricity supply, housing the system's main on-off switch and fuses or circuit breakers protecting individual circuits.

Cylinder A storage tank for hot water, supplied in most systems by cold water from a storage cistern in the loft. It contains a heat exchanger linked to a boiler, or an electric immersion heater.

Damp-proof course A strip of impervious material, formerly slate but nowadays of strong plastic, incorporated into walls just above ground level to prevent rising damp.

Damp-proof membrane A layer of impervious material incorporated in the structure of a solid ground floor to prevent rising damp.

Datum point A reference from which levels and other measurements are taken when setting out a site for a building or other construction work.

Fascia Horizontal planks on edge, nailed to the ends of the roof rafters at the eaves and carrying the gutters. If the rafters project beyond the wall, a soffit board fills the gap between the fascia and the house wall.

Feed-and-expansion tank A small water storage tank used to top up losses in vented central heating systems, and to accommodate expansion in the water volume as the system heats up; also called the header tank.

Fireback A shaped fireclay moulding forming the back of a fireplace opening. The components sit on the hearth and are linked to the flue above by a shaped mortar slope, forming a throat.

Flashing A strip of waterproof material – usually of lead, zinc or felt – used to waterproof the join between a roof slope and another adjacent surface (usually vertical, such as a chimney stack).

Footing A narrow concrete strip foundation for a wall.

Gatevalve A valve fitted to a low-pressure pipe run to allow it to be isolated from the supply for maintenance.

Gully An in-ground collection point for water from indoor appliances and downpipes. It contains an inverted trap to prevent drain smells from entering the house. Formerly earthenware, now usually plastic.

Hardcore Broken bricks and other masonry used to form a stable sub-base beneath paving, foundation slabs etc.

Head plate The top horizontal member of a timber-framed partition wall, fixed to the ceiling joists.

Inspection chamber An in-ground chamber installed on drain runs where the run changes direction or where a branch drain joins the main run. Formerly constructed of brickwork, those on house drains are now usually plastic.

Joist A horizontal wooden or metal beam used to support a floor, ceiling or upper wall. Steel beams with an I cross-section are usually called rolled steel joists (RSJs).

Junction box lighting circuits Circuits wired by running cable to a series of junction boxes, each of which is then wired to a light fitting and its switch.

Keystone The central brick or wedge-shaped stone at the top of an arch.

Lath and plaster A wall or ceiling finish formed by nailing slim laths to the underside of floor joists or the face of wall studs, and then covering the laths with plaster. It has been superseded by plasterboard.

Lintel A beam spanning a door or window opening, made from timber, natural stone, reinforced concrete or steel and supporting the wall above the opening.

Loop-in lighting circuits Circuits wired by running cable to each light position in turn. The switch cable is connected directly to the rose or the fitting it controls.

Mono-pitch roof A roof sloping in one direction only, better known as a lean-to roof.

Motorised valve An electrically powered control valve used on modern heating systems to divert the flow of water to individual parts (or zones) on the system.

Mullion A vertical member of a window frame fitted to divide the frame up into a number of separate fixed or opening lights.

Needle A stout supporting beam used with props to support the weight of a wall above a projected opening before a lintel or beam is inserted to carry the load.

Newel post The main vertical timbers used in staircase construction carrying the outer string and handrails and supporting them at an end or corner of the flight.

Nogging A short horizontal brace fitted between the studs of a timber-framed partition wall, or between ceiling joists

to provide fixing points for light fittings and other suspended fixtures.

One-pipe system A house drainage system in which soil and waste water from all appliances runs to the drains through one pipe. Separate vent pipes prevent traps from being siphoned out. Now generally replaced by single-stack systems.

Partition wall A wall between two rooms, non-loadbearing and generally just one storey high. It is often timber-framed, and clad with lath and plaster in older properties or with plasterboard in more recent ones.

Pebbledash An exterior wall finish created by throwing clean washed stones on to the freshly applied final rendering coat and pushing them in.

Plasterboard A building board made by sandwiching an aerated gypsum plaster core between two sheets of stout paper. It is universally used for lining partition walls and ceilings.

Plasticiser A chemical additive for mortar or concrete used to increase its plasticity and enabling the water content of the mix to be reduced.

Rendering A thin layer of cement-based mortar applied like plaster to external walls to create a protective finish. It may have small stones mixed into the render (roughcast) or bedded into it (pebbledash).

Reveal The vertical side of a recessed door or window opening in a wall.

Ring main circuits Power circuits wired as a continuous

ring, with both ends of the circuit connected to the same fuseway in the consumer unit.

Rising main The incoming mains pressure water supply pipe, which enters the house from below ground and rises to the storage cistern in the loft.

Screed A thin layer of mortar spread on a concrete floor or other surface to create a smooth finish.

Single-stack system A modern house drainage system where all soil and waste pipes discharge into a single large-diameter stack pipe. Deep-seal traps on waste pipes to appliances avoid the need for vent pipes.

Sleeper wall A low brick wall built to provide intermediate support for the joists of a suspended timber ground floor.

Soakaway A rubble-filled pit designed to accept rainwater from downpipes and help its dispersal into the sub-soil.

Soffit A board that is fitted between a fascia board and the house wall to close off projecting eaves.

Sole plate The horizontal base plate of a timber-framed partition wall, fixed to the floor off which the partition is built.

Stoptap A tap fitted to a mains-pressure supply pipe to regulate the flow rate and to allow the supply to be shut off for maintenance or repairs.

String One of the boards which form the angled sides of a flight of stairs, linking the two floors and providing support for the treads and risers. A wall string is fixed to a wall, and an open string is

free-standing. Both may be closed strings, with treads and risers in housings; the outer tread may be cut to follow the line of the treads and risers.

Stud A vertical member in a timber-framed partition wall fitting between the head and sole plates.

Transom A horizontal bar separating individual lights in a casement window frame, or between a door opening and a fanlight above it.

Trap An inverted loop of pipework or other similar device fitted to the waste outlet of all water-using appliances to prevent drain smells from entering the house. Modern plastic traps can be unscrewed for cleaning.

Two-way switching An arrangement allowing one light fitting to be controlled by two switches, which are linked by three-core and earth cable.

Vapour barrier A membrane such as polythene sheeting incorporated into a structure to prevent the passage of moisture-laden air – for example into a loft, or into external walls that are built of timber-frame construction.

Vent pipe A safety feature on heating and hot water systems that discharges any overheated water safely back into the storage cistern or feed-and-expansion tank.

Wall plate A horizontal timber bearer set on top of a wall to provide a fixing ground for the ends of floor or ceiling joists and also to spread their load.

Index